Steve Cuss started in the video games industry in 1994 as a programmer at Intelligent Games, rising to Development Director/co-owner after an MBO. At Intelligent Games Steve worked with Electronic Arts on franchises such as *Tiger Woods* and *FIFA* and with Sony on *World Tour Golf*.

Steve joined EA in 2001, working initially on the *Harry Potter* franchise. He moved to Criterion in 2003, working on *Black*, the *Burnout* series, *Need for Speed Most Wanted & Hot Pursuit*, *Star Wars Battlefront*, *Battlefield V: Firestorm* and *Need For Speed Unbound*. He became Head of Studio Operations in the summer of 2018 and that year was a Nominee for UK's Best Boss in the gamesindustry.biz annual awards.

Steve has spoken about Liberated Leadership at conferences in London, Manaus, Kiev and San Francisco.

Steve is married with two children and lives in Surrey, England.

For Rachel, Daniel and Joel.

Steve J. Cuss

LIBERATED LEADERSHIP

Unmasking The Authentic Leader Within

AUSTIN MACAULEY PUBLISHERS™

LONDON • CAMBRIDGE • NEW YORK • SHARJAH

A CIP catalogue record for this title is available from the British Library.

ISBN 9781035863044 (Paperback)
ISBN 9781035863341 (Hardback)
ISBN 9781035863051 (ePub e-book)

www.austinmacauley.com

First Published 2024
Austin Macauley Publishers Ltd®
1 Canada Square
Canary Wharf
London
E14 5AA

Table of Contents

When the ancient Masters said,
"If you want to become whole,
then first let yourself be broken,"
they weren't using empty words.
All who do this will be made complete.

Tao Te Ching Chapter 22 translated by **JH McDonald**.

About This Book

Listen, my friend, I've got something important to share with you. It's a secret that not many folks talk about, especially in the business world. You see, there's a whole bunch of leaders out there who wake up every morning and put on a mask. They transform into their work selves, playing a role they think they're supposed to play. It's like they're living a double life. But let me tell you, it's not easy to keep up this charade.

Behind that mask, these leaders face some serious challenges. They can't catch a decent night's sleep, and anxiety weighs them down day in and day out. Their energy levels go up and down like a yo-yo, and they feel exhausted most of the time. To keep going, they rely on copious amounts of coffee and quick meals that offer convenience but not much nourishment. It's a tough gig.

And it's not just their professional lives that suffer. These leaders carry the weight of their businesses on their shoulders, constantly worrying about their success. At the same time, their personal lives take a hit too. The balance between work and family? Well, it's completely lopsided, with work taking the lion's share. It's a struggle, my friend.

You know why I can speak about this? Because I've been there. I've lived that life, wearing the mask day in and day out. But let me tell you, it took a toll on me. The stress, the exhaustion—it all led me down a dark path of depression. I reached a breaking point and had to make some serious changes in how I approached life and leadership.

In the pages of this book, I'm sharing my journey with you. Over three decades in the video game industry, including a good chunk of time at Electronic Arts, I experienced firsthand how my traditional leadership style weighed me down. But don't worry; it's not all doom and gloom. Along the way, I discovered a new, healthier way to lead, and I call it liberated leadership.

Through my experiences, I'll introduce you to the seven pillars that are at the core of this liberated leadership style. Each pillar has its own key practice. These pillars and practices will empower you to lead people and projects in a way that's authentic and fulfilling. And here's the best part—they pave the way for a whole new change cycle, helping you break free from the chains that have held you back.

So, my friend, if you're ready to shed that mask, let go of the burdens, and embark on a journey of liberation, this book is for you. I'll be your guide, sharing practical advice and insights that can transform your approach to life and leadership. It's time to set yourself and those you lead free. Let's walk this path together.

Introduction

Back in September 2012, I found myself sitting in Dr Cantopher's office at The Priory Hospital in Woking, England. As I shared my life history and relationships, I couldn't help but notice that my profile didn't match that of a typical depression sufferer. It was puzzling, but the fact remained—I couldn't perform my role as a video game producer, and I felt lost, devoid of joy and hope.

In that precise moment, reality hit me like a tonne of bricks. It was time to face the truth—I was actually ill. Until then, I had been grappling with internal doubts, questioning whether I was just making things up or being weak. But here I was, sitting in the office of Dr Tim Cantopher, a respected consultant psychiatrist who had just confirmed that I had depression. I couldn't ignore it any longer.

My journey through depression has been a whirlwind of contradictions and paradoxes. On one hand, I was anxious about seeing a psychiatrist, as I carried out a lurking belief that I was a fraud and simply weak, rather than someone battling an illness. I thought maybe an expert in the field of psychiatric medicine would confirm my doubts. Yet, there was another part of me that was strangely excited about meeting Dr Cantopher. You see, four years prior, I had read England cricketer Marcus Trescothick's book, 'Coming Back to Me,' which chronicled his journey with depression. Little did I know that depression was something that could affect me too. Marcus mentioned how Dr Cantopher's book, 'The Curse of the Strong', helped him realise he might be ill and that there could be a cure. Intrigued, I bought a copy for myself, thinking it would be useful knowledge if I ever encountered someone struggling with depression. I never imagined I would need it as a self-help guide. It's funny how life works, isn't it?

Just a few weeks prior to that moment, I was standing on the grand stage of Gamescom, presenting the highly anticipated game, Need for Speed Most Wanted, to the world. Gamescom, along with E3, is one of the biggest trade events in the gaming industry. It was an intense experience, with back-to-back interviews, live streams, and demonstrations. But here's the thing—no one watching those interviews would have guessed that I was teetering on the edge of what was once called a "nervous breakdown," and is now commonly known as "nervous exhaustion." You see, many depression sufferers become masters at masking their pain, and I had become quite skilled at acting the part of a composed leader.

So why couldn't I admit to myself how dire things had become? Despite overwhelming evidence staring me in the face, I existed in a perpetual state of anxiety—a relentless combination of mental agony and physical pain. My mind was constantly on high alert, searching for any potential pitfalls that could jeopardise our game's success. The pressure became unbearable, and I longed for an escape. I often found myself scrutinising my personal finances, desperately trying to convince myself that I could walk away from work. But deep down, my self-esteem had plummeted so low that I couldn't fathom anyone wanting to hire me again if I left my current job. Sleep became a fleeting luxury, with alcohol and exhaustion being my lullabies. Yet, I would often wake up in the wee hours of the morning, my mind racing, engrossed in the same problem-solving frenzy from the previous day.

I still vividly recall the breaking point. This happened during a meeting to prioritise the final polish tasks for our nearly complete version of Need for Speed Most Wanted. We were working tirelessly, trying to meet project deadlines. It was common practice in the industry to push ourselves to the limit to finish a game. But this time, something within me snapped. My heart raced, and my mind raced even faster. As I looked around the room, searching for some connection, I suggested an idea—a feature to enhance the end game. And just like that, it was rejected. It wasn't an unusual occurrence in game development, as we often discarded valuable ideas for the sake of progress. But this time, it felt different. It was as if a dam had burst inside my mind. I couldn't hear what others were saying; it was as if my ears were filled with water.

Overwhelmed and drained of energy, I couldn't even lift myself from my chair, even if the room were engulfed in flames. And though I felt like I was falling apart, no one in the room seemed to notice. I felt numb and detached from my anxiety. At that moment, I realised something was seriously wrong with me.

I didn't know what to do with this realisation. At the time, I didn't have a name for it. So, I continued with my usual routine, going for a walk with a coworker through the gardens near Guildford Castle. It was during that walk, amidst the vibrant colours of carefully manicured flowers, that the truth hit me when Alan simply asked, "Are you alright?" I finally considered the question honestly and I was far from "Alright." I had to stop pretending. We walked back to the office, and I mustered the courage to speak to my manager. I confessed that I couldn't continue and that I was burned out. To their eternal credit, EA supported me fully, telling me to hand over my phone and laptop and take as much time as I needed to recover. And as I left the building in a daze, detached from my own actions, I couldn't help but feel guilty for leaving my friends to carry on without me.

When the diagnosis finally came, it was a mix of shock and relief. "Okay," I said to myself, "you're actually ill. But you know what? You're going to be damn good at getting well." There I was, in that moment where perfectionism had broken me down, silently making a pact with myself to be perfect in my journey towards recovery. I had so much to learn.

This is the story of my illumination—a glimpse into the depths of my battle with depression. It's a testament to resilience, growth, and the pursuit of understanding mental health. Join me on this voyage of liberation, where knowledge is gained, stigmas are challenged, and the power of healing shines bright and where I find a new way to lead and a new way to live.

Part 1
Leading Myself into Trouble

Who's Responsible? I'm Responsible

Depression is a PHYSICAL illness. "It is every bit as physical as pneumonia or a broken leg." In depression, the bit that's broken is called the `Limbic System'. Only STRONG people are at risk of developing depression. This physical illness does not develop out of the blue, or caught like a cold; it develops after prolonged periods of pushing yourself too hard, and/or experiencing a major life-event or series of life-events. Everyone who has had, or will have depression shares something in common—a conscientious personality, with a drive to keep going and never giving up. Weak/lazy people never get up and get started, average people have the ability to say—stop, enough is enough; but the highly conscientious don't know when to quit until it's too late, then depression sets in and everything falls apart.

Curse of the Strong—Dr Tim Cantopher.

I grew up with a deep passion for sports, especially football. During my time in primary school, you would always find me and my friends playing football during break and lunchtime on the concrete playground. We dreamt of the day when we could move to the grass field for bigger games. After school and on weekends, we would gather at a local field for our own "big matches." Football was a major part of our lives.

At the age of nine, I eagerly awaited the opportunity to play my first proper, organised match with a kit and a referee. Little did I know that chance would come sooner than expected. One day, Mr Parker, another teacher, called me out of class. I was thrilled to discover that he had arranged a game for our year against a nearby school. Without a second thought, I stepped into the role of team selector, effortlessly listing the names of my classmates and positioning myself in centre midfield, right at the heart of the action. My best friends, David and Mark, became the forwards. As the day of the game arrived, it felt natural for me to take on the role of team captain, exchanging handshakes with the opposing captain and calling the coin toss with the referee. It was simply what I did at the time, embracing the responsibility of leadership. I can still vividly remember that game—a rollercoaster of emotions as we went one-nil up, fell behind two-one, and eventually equalised. I even wrote about it for the school magazine, something I considered my duty without question.

This pattern continued throughout secondary school. I was the captain of the football, basketball, cricket, and athletic teams. In university, I joined the basketball club and served as the social secretary for my first and second years before taking on the role of team captain in my final year. Reflecting on those teams, I may not have been the most talented player, but teachers and peers saw me as a natural choice for leadership. It was a responsibility I gladly embraced.

This attitude extended to almost anything I was involved in. I was called for jury duty on four occasions, always stepping forward or allowing myself to be convinced to take on the role of the jury's leader. In group workshops, I automatically assumed the responsibility of providing feedback on behalf of the entire group.

Over time, I've come to realise that there is a unique relationship between my willingness to take on responsibility and others' inclination to bestow it upon me. This combination often characterises someone seen as a natural leader but also makes them highly susceptible to overload and potential burnout.

Consider this table:

	LOW willingness to take responsibility	HIGH willingness to take responsibility
HIGH willingness of others to bestow responsibility	**Reluctant Leaders**	**"Natural" Leaders**
LOW willingness of others to bestow responsibility	**Happy Contributors**	**Aspiring Leaders**

Being described as a 'natural leader' may sound like a compliment, but from my experience, it can be a precarious position to be in. The ease with which responsibility flows onto such an individual increases the risk of exceeding their capacity. A contented contributor may be propelled into a leadership role by circumstances, while a reluctant leader may be nudged by those around them.

However, their hesitancy to embrace more responsibilities could very well be a defence mechanism against overwhelming themselves in leadership positions.

Jack of all trades, master of…all of them, all of them, I'm going to master all of them.

No matter what I pursued in my youth, I had an expectation of mastering it. Whether it was trying out different sports or delving into various subjects, I always aimed for excellence. Whenever there were school plays, I anticipated landing the lead role, and when it came to sixth form shows, I expected it to be the compère. Through a combination of natural talent and hard work, I often achieved success. I also believe that what we expect to happen in any given situation is often what is most likely to occur. However, I was completely unaware of the psychological trap I was unknowingly setting for myself—I had unconsciously set perfection as my minimum standard.

When the time came to choose a degree to study at university, it felt natural for me to pursue my interests in Computer Science and Drama. To others, it may have seemed like an unlikely combination, but it suited me perfectly. I had already learned how to code during a gap year after completing my A-Levels while working for IBM in Winchester, which made the computer science aspect of my course relatively straightforward.

Drama, on the other hand, was more of a personal passion. During my summers, I divided my time between working for a company that developed air traffic control simulators and taking student shows to the Edinburgh Fringe Festival. Surprisingly, these experiences proved to be excellent preparation for a career in the video game industry, where the fusion of science and art is crucial in creating entertaining experiences.

When I graduated in 1992, I had an offer to study Theatre Direction. However, considering the considerable debt I had accumulated, I made the decision to take a full-time job at the simulation company. During my time there, which spanned a couple of years, I gained valuable insights into working as part of a team in software development. I also learned C++, as it was a requirement for securing a job in the games industry at that time.

Around 1995, at the same time that Criterion was established as a subsidiary of Canon research, I stumbled upon an advertisement in The Guardian for a London startup called Intelligent Games (IG). I attended the interview in Chelsea, at a building opposite Bryan Adams' flat that had formerly served as The Rolling Stones' Fan Club HQ. I must admit, I may have been a tad overdressed for the occasion, as when I met Kevin, one of the co-owners at the time, he was casually sporting a reggae t-shirt. I fared well in the programming test, and when asked about my favourite game, I mentioned golf games. As luck would have it, IG had secured a contract from Electronic Arts to develop the PGA European Tour for PC, and I was the only interviewee who had expressed any interest in golf. The job was mine. Straight into the lead.

It's quite common for video games to be developed based on the code, artwork, and sound of another game. In the case of the PGA European Tour, we were tasked with creating the game based on PGA 96, which was still being developed by EA's team in San Mateo, California. We had to regularly receive updates from the American team until they had completed their game, which would be several months before our scheduled launch. Back in those days, we didn't have fast internet connections, so the updates would arrive by courier on a CD-ROM.

Our team consisted of three artists, two designers, and me as the programmer. We were all in our twenties. Our office space was far from ideal for game development—the floors were sloped, and we often lost work because someone would accidentally kick a power cable out of the wall by tripping over it. However, despite the challenges, I loved it. During our lunch breaks, we would head to the Bluebird Arcade cafeteria and rush back to play network games like Duke Nukem and Doom together. After work, we would walk over to The World's End pub on Kings Road to enjoy drinks as a team. Work wasn't just a means to earn an income for me; it was also like a second family.

It took us six months to develop that game, meticulously dissecting the game code to understand how it was constructed. It felt quite natural for me to devise the overall development plan for our small team, as well as for myself. Little did I know at the time that nothing would ever be as straightforward again.

Given my innate tendencies as a "natural leader," it seemed inevitable, and honestly not surprising, when I was asked to take on the role of team leader for my first game in addition to my programming responsibilities. In reality, I was already fulfilling that role. I had, in many ways, been "anointed more than appointed." I believe many people rise to leadership positions in a similar way, and it's a phrase that often arises when I'm coaching individuals today.

Adventures in Company Direction

After completing PGA European Tour, we continued our work with Electronic Arts on golf games, but more responsibility was coming my way. The founder of IG reached a point where he couldn't continue with the company. That's when my colleagues, Neil and Kevin, and I decided to step in and complete a management buy-out, becoming company directors. The terms of the buy-out didn't require us to invest cash into the company (at 24 and in my first job, I didn't have any), but rather, Neil, Kevin, and I had to provide personal guarantees for the company's overdraft. For me, it meant that if IG couldn't pay its debts, I would have to repay the bank a significant sum of fifty thousand pounds—nearly half the value of my house at the time. However, it seemed like a reasonable risk to take, especially considering that Electronic Arts had previously shown interest in acquiring our company.

IG was regularly profitable, working with Hasbro, Ocean Software, Cryo Interactive, BBC, Sony Psygnosis, and, of course, Electronic Arts.

However, we always operated on a cash flow basis. As directors, we were constantly chasing payments from our publishers to ensure we meet our monthly payroll. The responsibility I felt to ensure my friends and colleagues were paid each month was a constant pressure that gradually became insidiously stressful.

My personal response to the mounting pressure and stress was to take on more and more tasks and assume greater responsibility. This reached its peak when we worked on Pro 18–World Tour Golf for Sony Psygnosis. In addition to being a company director and handling the business negotiations, I found myself being the game designer, lead programmer, project planner, and manager of the entire team. Looking back, it was an absurd amount of responsibility to shoulder, but at the time, I didn't question it. Taking on multiple roles and responsibilities was the norm for me. I remember thinking that if I didn't step up as the lead programmer at that moment, I might never have the chance.

The consequences were inevitable. The project consumed me entirely, taking a toll on my physical health as I gained weight. Mentally, I struggled to sleep at night and started relying on alcohol as a sedative. My marriage suffered as I was physically present at home but emotionally absent, which was a rare occurrence. I distinctly remember one Sunday, when I was actually at home, receiving a phone call from our publishers notifying me that they had a full shift of QA testers arriving the next day, but we didn't have a build of the game ready for testing. Without hesitation, I drove to the office in Putney, created a new build of the game onto a CD, travelled by train to Liverpool, and then took a taxi to Sony Psygnosis' offices. I handed over the build to the lead tester at reception and retraced the entire journey back home.

My identity had become completely intertwined with that of the company. There was no separation. This lack of boundaries was incredibly unhealthy, as my moods fluctuated with the state of the company, which was highly volatile.

At that time, IG took on two types of projects, typical of an independent game developer. The first involved 'advances versus royalties' deals, similar to those used in the music and book publishing industries. A publisher would provide the developer with an advance payment, which was used to fund the game's development. The developer would then earn royalties as a percentage of the publisher's profit from the game, receiving payment once their share of the royalties exceeded the initial advance. The second type of project involved 'work-for-hire' agreements. In this case, the developer would create part or all of a game for the publisher and receive a predetermined fee for their services, with no royalties involved. Payment for the work-for-hire projects or the advance payments for royalties were usually tied to specific deliverables or milestones. As a developer, we had to estimate the costs of our staff and overheads required to complete the work and negotiate a price that would yield a profit—our margin. Typically, we could negotiate a higher margin on work-for-hire agreements, as there was no guarantee of future income once the game was released. Thus, we had to carefully manage the risk versus reward when signing contracts. Would we opt for a higher-risk, lower-margin development for the possibility of higher rewards through potential royalties?

The business model of an independent developer like ours usually relied on generating enough income and margin from work-for-hire projects to balance the risks associated with lower-margin advances versus royalties deals. As directors, our exit strategy hinged on either creating a massive hit that generated significant royalties or being acquired by one of the publishers for whom we provided development services.

Despite being a profitable business and experiencing year-on-year growth, the old saying 'cash is king' was particularly relevant to IG. The company's operations were driven by cash flow. We relied on payments from our game publishers to sustain our development services. These payments were often linked to specific milestones in the development process, and whether we received them or not was subject to the subjective judgement of the publisher's producer overseeing the project. I expended a great deal of energy negotiating with these producers, ensuring that milestones were deemed complete and, even more importantly, chasing payments within the typical 90-day terms.

Despite all the pressures, we managed to grow our company's turnover successfully, and it seemed that selling the company might not be the best exit strategy. So, we decided to increase our risk further and explore the possibility of independently raising funds for one of our game projects. Self-funding a project had the potential for much greater rewards, as it allowed us to retain the intellectual property rights and the majority of the royalties. However, the absence of external development funding also introduced a significant increase in risk. This further intensified the pressure on our work-for-hire projects.

Unfortunately, during that time, our main work-for-hire projects were with a publisher called Bay Area Media (BAM). At one point, BAM suddenly ceased paying us for any of our completed milestones. It turned out that they were facing their own financial difficulties, but their failure to pay us was a devastating blow. I distinctly remember the sickening feeling when the directors gathered with our financial controller one early morning, and he uttered those words: "We're insolvent. If you sign one more cheque, you will be breaking the law." It forced us to put the company into a Creditors Voluntary Agreement (CVA).

I found myself in a state of numbness, but the realisation that we would have to inform all our staff shook me out of it. It was one of the worst days of my life. They had worked so hard for us, and now we had to inform them that they were out of a job and, even worse, that they wouldn't receive payment for that month's work. We made the decision that one of the three directors would personally inform each employee as they arrived for work. By ten o'clock, a few had already arrived at the office. The responses varied greatly—anger, distress, disbelief— but there were also genuine acts of compassion toward us as directors. Some even offered to continue working for free, hoping that we could somehow recover. I felt an immense sense of guilt, punishing myself with the thought that I had let them all down. However, once the CVA was in place, we were no longer directors of the company, and like them, I had to start looking for a new job.

How to Make a Video Game

Before I delve into my journey in the games industry, I believe it would be worthwhile to explain the process of creating a video game, as I understand that our approach is often shrouded in mystery for those outside the industry. When I meet someone for the first time and the conversation turns to my profession, I often encounter one of two reactions to my answer of "I make video games." The first response is usually, "Oh, it must be fantastic to play games all day," while the second typically involves a question like, "So, how does it all happen? Does someone just come up with an idea and then…?" The question tends to trail off. So, allow me to provide a brief overview of the people involved in the game development team and how we collaborate.

Developers, Developers, Developers

In my opinion, game development represents some of the most intricate software development work happening today. No other industry combines creativity and science quite like game development, and this is reflected in the diverse skill sets found within a typical AAA game team. Furthermore, while most commercial software projects are considered long-term if they span a few months, game development is characterised by projects lasting two years or more, with some original ventures extending to seven years or beyond.

Within a typical game team, you'll encounter individuals with backgrounds in both the arts and sciences, along with a mix of individuals who thrive in associative and logical thinking.

	ARTS Education	SCIENCE Education
SEQUENTIAL Thinking	**3D Artists** **Technical Artists** **Level Designers**	**Systems Engineers** **Development Directors** **Quality Assurance**
ASSOCIATIVE Thinking	**Audio Designers** **Art Directors** **2D Graphic Artists**	**Gameplay Engineers** **Designers** **Customer Experience** **Producers**

Throughout the years, I have had the privilege of meeting and collaborating with numerous talented developers. I've observed distinct traits in the various crafts required to create a game, and I have great admiration for each of them. I have learned invaluable lessons from their expertise. Allow me to paint a portrait of each craft based on my experiences.

Engineers (Also Known As Programmers or Coders)

As someone who started my journey as an engineer, this group is perhaps the easiest for me to comprehend. This is also the group I have had the most direct management experience with. Typically, a game team engineer begins their coding journey as a self-taught teenager and later pursues a degree in computer science or mathematics. Interestingly, many of them also have a knack for playing the guitar.

Fundamentally, engineers work with logic and excel at creating intricate systems. They are not easily swayed by abstract arguments. It's not that they don't understand these arguments; rather, they are not easily moved by them. When I need to influence a group of engineers, I know I must present a fully developed, logically coherent argument that begins with observation, clearly states objectives, outlines implementation plans, and includes methods for testing against established success criteria.

When seeking feedback from engineers, especially regarding process or strategy changes, it's crucial to recognise that their input is rooted in locating and rectifying any errors in your proposal. In other words, they approach it as debugging. This might appear as disagreement, but making such an assumption would be perilous. Additionally, keep in mind that engineers will respond to the exact question you ask, even if it's not precisely what you intended. Therefore, precision in communication is essential. For example, asking "do you like this idea?" may elicit a different response than "do you think we should pursue this?"

Artists

A typical artist in a game team would have been captivated by the visual allure of games from an early age, although not all of them would have initially pursued fine art skills like "drawing from the elbow." A significant portion of game art production involves technical proficiency, and I have encountered several talented 3D artists with science degrees, such as physics.

Artists are generally more influenced by intuition and emotion than strict logic. The prevailing atmosphere within a group can exert a strong impact. The manner in which a proposal is presented can significantly affect its likelihood of acceptance.

Professional game artists have learned to navigate the inherent anxiety surrounding the quality of their artwork. Most of them never truly feel deep down that their work is complete; they always aspire to improve it. Hence, when asked, "how long will it take you to create this?" the typical response from a video game artist is, "how much time do I have?" Skilfully managing the time allocated for art production is one of the most effective ways for production leaders to support the success of artists.

Sound Designers (Also Known As Audio Artists)

These individuals are musicians within the team, often proficient in playing multiple instruments to a high standard. In my experience, they are the group most resistant to categorisation. Many stumbled into the field, unaware that a career in video game development was open to musicians. Some initially aspired to work in the film industry. Much of what sound designers do overlaps with the role of a movie foley artist. All of them tend to possess extraordinary levels of creativity.

Game Designers

Understanding game designers involves recognising that game design has been the last of the crafts to establish a formal educational path through university. Even today, degrees in game design offer no guarantee of entry into the industry, as they are viewed with scepticism by game studios whose leaders grew up in a time before such degrees existed. Consequently, many current game designers began their careers in other roles within game development. Some started as engineers, discovering their aptitude for designing gameplay systems while working on code. Others began as sound designers, and a few (although less common in my experience) began as artists. However, the largest group of game designers started their journey as game testers. For those without an immediate affinity for other game development crafts, testing (or quality assurance, QA) is often the gateway. Identifying flaws in a game during development provides valuable training in understanding how a game comes together.

Producers and Development Directors

Within EA gambling, producers, and development directors (DDs) hold distinct roles. However, in other parts of the industry, these responsibilities are combined into one position known as the producer. These roles are fulfilled by the leaders in production. They must plan, prioritise, measure, and readjust. They inspire, motivate, and influence the team. They manage project budgets and represent the commercial interests of those funding development. Increasingly, they employ data analytics to assess game usability and its appeal to target player motivations.

In EA game teams, DDs serve as professional project managers. They possess expertise in processes and have studied methodologies such as Kanban, Agile, and Waterfall. I will elaborate on these methodologies and their differences in the following section. Producers excel in prioritising and advocating for player motivation and business needs during development. To illustrate the distinction between a producer and a DD, a producer might say things like, "Right now, the most crucial focus for us is refining the race experience," or "That's a great idea, but it's not suitable for the current phase." On the other hand, a DD might be heard discussing achievements such as, "We accomplished 70% of our milestone goals," or "Based on the latest trend data, here is the number of features we anticipate achieving by the launch date."

I have assumed both roles, and at times, to the detriment of my own well-being, attempted to juggle both simultaneously.

People Managers

While some teams have dedicated people managers, in most cases, people management responsibilities fall upon individuals who already have another role. I believe this is one of the most crucial yet often under-recognised roles within a game team. Gerald Weinberg, a renowned author of numerous books on programming processes, famously wrote a line I frequently quote: "No matter what they tell you, it's always a people problem."

I appreciate the fact that this observation comes from an author focused on the engineering process, which is the most logical of the crafts. Recruiting the right mix of talented individuals, fostering diversity, and enabling effective collaboration is the greatest challenge in game development. The feedback and guidance provided by dedicated and empathetic people managers are essential for keeping team members engaged and motivated. However, this aspect is often overlooked. We seldom consider who coached a successful individual, but when issues arise and someone is underperforming or displaying improper behaviour, others begin to question who manages that person.

There's a Method in the Madness

All these talented individuals require a process to integrate their efforts and create a polished game.

When I first started planning video game production in the mid-1990s, I adopted a waterfall approach. This approach originates from the manufacturing of physical goods and the construction industry. It is a linear method where tasks follow a predetermined sequence. Similar to building a house, we begin with the foundations, then the superstructure, and so on. In waterfalls, task dependencies are well-defined. For instance, we cannot construct the roof until the walls are completed. This sequential nature gives it the name "waterfall method." It is often said that in a waterfall approach, going back to a previous stage is not possible, as you can't push water uphill. However, a more accurate statement is that going back a stage is undesirable and costly. If we discover inadequate foundations after completing the superstructure of a house, we must tear down everything and start anew.

Certain aspects of game development may make the waterfall approach appear suitable. There are consistent phases a game project goes through, such as Concept, Pre-production, Production, Finalising, Launch, Live Service, and Sunsetting. However, even when I used the waterfall approach, it was evident to me that our success stemmed from adapting the process to our specific needs, rather than using it off-the-shelf. The most apparent indicator of this was the constant need for replanning the remaining waterfall towards the project's end, as changes arose from various sources: alterations to game design, under estimated tasks that emerged, tools improving or causing re-estimation of work, and playing completed parts of the game and discovering areas that lacked fun. This required building extensive Gannt charts in Microsoft Projects but manipulating them to work in ways they were not designed for, essentially recalculating the project as if it restarted with each change.

Waterfall is fundamentally ineffective when requirements for the project are not fully known at the beginning, and it was clear to me that in game development, many requirements emerged during the game's development process. By the early 2000s, I, along with the majority of the gaming industry, transitioned towards embracing some form of Agile development. While Waterfall is a structured approach, Agile is renowned for its flexibility. This follows an incremental rather than sequential approach, allowing for changes in requirements during development.

Agile development is characterised by its expectation of changing and evolving requirements. This entails continuous iterations of development and testing in the software development process. Agile methodology can be summarised in these steps:

Build the next version of the software that provides valuable learning (an iteration).
Review and test the software iteration.
Adapt the plan based on the insights gained from the review.
Repeat the process.

Implementing an Agile approach presents several challenges compared to Waterfall:

- It requires an expert to be available to make crucial decisions when individuals are carrying out work that requires guidance, as delays may occur otherwise.
- Educating the entire team is crucial when implementing Agile, as everyone is involved in project management decisions.

32

- Without a clear outcome in mind, an Agile project can easily deviate from its intended path if the project manager lacks clarity in their objectives.

Baking a Game

A compelling analogy for game development is likening it to preparing a Michelin-star banquet for discerning customers. Just as there is no room for hiding mistakes within a kitchen crew, the same holds true for a game development team. The ingredients in a game, such as the art, audio, and gameplay code, must be fresh and of the utmost quality. While the game team produces much of its content internally, it also relies on suppliers in cost-effective locations like China. Similar to a kitchen, the workspace in which the team operates, represented by game engines, must meet the highest standards and accommodate all team members. Sometimes, innovations like the creation of sous vide cooking can provide a competitive advantage, attracting customers over other offerings. In game development, teams may create their own game engine, the foundational code that allows for the creation and rendering of core assets like characters and the game world. However, it is increasingly common for teams to utilise engines developed by third parties such as Unity or Unreal. EA has even developed its own engine called Frostbite. It is worth noting that while some may correlate the quality of a game with the quality of its technology, I believe that a bad game can be made with exceptional technology and vice versa, much like a skilled chef can create a remarkable meal in a subpar kitchen, and vice versa.

The head chef and their leadership team, akin to the game's leadership team, are responsible for crafting recipes that surprise and delight customers, much like game designs do. These recipes must be feasible for the talented team to execute within the allotted time and budget, ultimately generating profits for the business. Leading a Michelin-star restaurant or a world-class game team demands an all-consuming commitment from passionate individuals dedicated to their craft.

Burnout and Crash

I joined EA in 2002, and after two years, I moved to Criterion. It was an exciting time as we were in the midst of developing Black, while Burnout Revenge had recently been completed for Sony's PlayStation 2 and Microsoft's Xbox consoles, which were known as the 'sixth generation' of video game consoles.

During the sixth generation, a typical game team consisted of around 50–60 people. The Burnout team, who had just finished working on Burnout Revenge, was a mix of the skillsets I described in Chapter 2.

The initial project where I assumed a leadership role involved the adaptation of Burnout Revenge for Microsoft's Xbox 360 console. The endeavour commenced shortly after the console's launch in November 2005. Although the game we were working on was highly acclaimed, achieving an impressive Metacritic review score of 89, it became evident that the team I inherited was facing various challenges.

One of my initial tasks was to read and condense the 'postmortem' reviews that had been conducted for the previous project they had completed. These reviews served as a reflection of the development process and outcomes. I took it upon myself to gather insights from these reviews and present them back to the team in a cohesive manner. Here is a summary of what I reported,

Wins

- The team members had a strong drive for excellence and focused on delivering a high-quality game.
- Efforts to develop team members through initiatives like one-on-one meetings and personal development plans were initially recognised.

- Positive process aspects included regular team check-ins, a visible and accessible build machine, task forces, individual project area assignments for producers, rapid iteration, and peer code review.

Challenges

- Unstable build impacting design iteration on occasion.
- Communication was not always sufficiently clear.
- Review structure.
- Role descriptions not keeping pace with team evolution.
- Insufficient contingency planning.
- Process failures.
- Intense finishing period.

The team developed their own unique methodology, blending elements of both Waterfall and Agile. Their approach embraced the importance of an iterative process. For instance, they had devised a powerful pre-visualisation technique where a dedicated group of developers with animation and video editing skills utilised various software tools. This enabled the creative team to gain a quick understanding of the desired look and feel of a feature design without having to fully implement it in the game software. However, it became evident that their approach lacked the structured rituals and progress estimation practices outlined in the formal Agile methodology. Therefore, the team had to invent these practices themselves.

Iterative methodologies, whether Agile or the team's own approach, thrive in situations where time and funding are flexible. However, they can introduce additional stress when working with fixed-price scenarios. In the case of Burnout Revenge, similar to much of the industry, there came a point where the leaders felt they had committed to delivering the game by a specific launch date, maintaining a quality standard that nobody wanted to compromise. Beyond this point, development effectively became fixed in terms of both price and time, which inevitably created considerable stress when new requirements continued to emerge.

Looking back now, I would have been more mindful of the significance of the intensity with which the team had been working. Although it was, and still is, common for groups of young, talented people to work intensively on creative projects, this particular project had clearly been something of a watershed for leaders and developers alike, causing them to wonder about the way they were working. There was an opportunity to move on to an approach that served everyone better, but at that stage, with the mindset I was in, I just joined in with the intensity.

Burnout

The problem with roles is the unconscious commitments we make when we take them on.
Conscious Loving by Gay and Kathlyn Hendricks.

Let me make this perfectly clear: I do not blame anyone for me getting ill. To do that would leave me in a victim's space. By owning the responsibility for getting ill, I keep the power to be well and be the person I choose to be. My decisions and choices brought me to the point of illness, and at this point I had brought myself into a position, ironically, while working on a game called Burnout, that set me on the path to burn out.

As we embarked on the development of Burnout 5, which would later be known as Burnout Paradise and be released in 2008, challenges mounted both personally and for the team.

The traditional way of operating, with its attempts to scale up the existing workflow, began to reveal its flaws. The cracks in the system became more pronounced as we faced the demands of this ambitious project. It was a pivotal moment for Criterion, and the challenges we encountered served as a wake-up call. We needed to reassess our approach and find a more sustainable path forward.

At the start of the project, I moved into a production leadership role, managing the project plan. It meant I was responsible for how we delivered the game. I had developed the idea that a good way to get a quick feel for risk on a project was to count how many 'firsts' there are on the project. Things that the team would need to do for the project to be successful that they were doing for the first time. I later refined this list to grade 'firsts' at three levels of ascending risk:

1. A first for this team but not the company.
2. A first for this company but not the industry (and there is a public description of the technique or solution).
3. An industry first.

As we moved Burnout from a game where cars never left carefully designed tracks to one where players could drive freely around an open world, we encountered a number of 'firsts'. Firsts bring unknowns, and unknowns bring risk. It was my job as owner of the project plan to report on these risks and their impact on the project plan.

As luck would have it, just before I could attend that important meeting, a prolapsed disc in my back unexpectedly ruptured, leading me to undergo surgery and requiring me to rest in a prone position for several weeks, leaving me absent from work.

During my recovery, I had a phone conversation with my manager, who made the decision to switch roles with a project manager from another Criterion project that had a later shipping date. Interestingly, the other manager happened to be my friend, and this seemed like a sensible arrangement at the time.

However, upon my return to work, it became apparent that things were not as I had anticipated. There was no designated workspace for me for the other project, and it was my friend who had to deliver the disappointing news regarding Burnout 5. When I met with my manager, I was requested to compile a report, akin to an "air crash investigation," detailing what went wrong. Although it was never stated, I felt a sense of blame for the project's shortcomings. It became evident that I would not be leading the other project. Eventually, Jon took it upon himself to inform me that I would not be assuming the role and asked if I could assist him in a junior capacity on Burnout 5. Although not stated, I internalised a sense of blame, which, given my inclination to take responsibility, was all too easy for me to believe.

Furthermore, I believe I was coming from leadership meetings I had regularly attended prior to my back injury.

Interestingly, at the time, I never thought about exploring other opportunities. My attachment to the team and a misplaced sense of duty towards completing the game held me back. Instead, I decided to take on the responsibility of managing the graphics and tools team. Surprisingly, it turned out to be an exceptional team. Many of the individuals who joined Criterion during that time have since progressed to senior roles, successfully delivering remarkable games to our players. Working alongside these talented individuals was truly enjoyable.

However, despite the positive experience, my pride and self-confidence took a significant blow. I felt the weight of my previous setbacks, and the path to reclaiming a leadership position seemed daunting and distant. Nonetheless, I remained dedicated to my work and committed to regaining my confidence in due course.

I persevered in my junior role until an opportunity arose for me to take on a pivotal position as a Talent Manager Officer, responsible for overseeing the supply of talent to various game teams within EA in the UK. At the time, Criterion was working on Burnout, alongside the development of Harry Potter games and some exciting new original concepts. Unfortunately, the role turned out to be a disaster for me. It required extensive negotiation and conflict resolution, but my confidence to act on my judgement had been severely shaken, despite still believing in my abilities. I felt utterly miserable and isolated, no longer part of a game team but instead caught in the midst of conflicts with game team leaders. Desperation consumed me, and so I began to hate going to work.

I experienced restless sleep, waking up anxious and nauseous. There were instances where I had to pull over my car on the way to work just to retch and heave, despite having nothing left in my stomach. My credibility as a leader felt shattered, and though I didn't lose faith in my capabilities, my anxiety somehow severed the connection to take decisive action.

Fortunately, an opportunity for escape presented itself following the launch of Burnout Paradise. I was so low that I believed I would be let go; in fact, I was entrusted with a leadership role in managing aspects of the Paradise live service. During that time, the concept of supporting games with additional content and improvements post-launch was still novel. Being back on the game team, collaborating with colleagues I admired and enjoyed working with, revitalised my passion for game development. We introduced telemetry into our game, providing near-real-time reports on how it was being played, enabling us to respond swiftly. Some of the content we released was a direct response to observing player behaviour, while other ideas, such as the Toy Cars, stemmed from our team's creative thinking.

Following a year of supporting Burnout Paradise, we embarked on a project that would become Need for Speed Hot Pursuit, with a planned release date of November 2010. Building on the relationships I had forged during Paradise, I worked closely with a team focused on our online features, which later became known as Autolog. It was an exceptional team, and we steadily made progress towards creating something truly captivating. Drawing on the Agile project management philosophy and framework I learned during Burnout Paradise, I applied many of its principles to Hot Pursuit. I formed a strong partnership with Matt Webster, whom I had known and collaborated with since the beginning of my career, as he served as the EA Producer of PGA European Tour.

As was customary in the industry at the time, we worked intensively towards the final stages of the project. However, compared to some of our past projects, we considered it relatively manageable. The game achieved significant success and even won a BAFTA for Best Online Play. It was a proud moment to walk on stage at the prestigious black-tie awards ceremony in London, collecting the award with my teammates in the presence of members of the band Blue.

On the back of this success, I was promoted back into an overall project leadership role. Things seemed to be back on track, and I felt that my anxiety and stress levels were under control. Little did I know on that joyous day what challenges lay ahead.

During that period, we were putting in a lot of effort to embrace an Agile approach. We had daily team meetings and implemented burndown charts to track our progress. However, we encountered some major hurdles along the way. Our decision-making process was sluggish, and the team struggled to adapt quickly to shifting priorities. These challenges posed significant obstacles to our journey towards true agility.

The root cause of this was how we were leading the projects. The core change cycle on the project had not really changed from the one we evolved when we started making games in the 1990s. It looked like this.

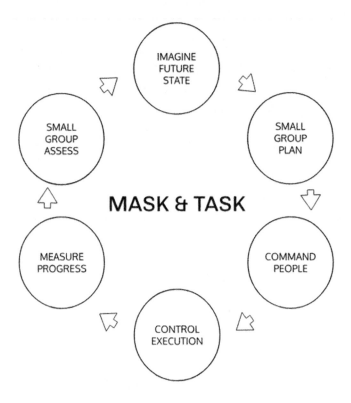

In our studio, a small group of senior leaders played a key role in assessing our game's progress. We had various metrics to measure productivity, such as sprint burndowns and throughput measures. However, evaluating the ultimate goal of creating a fun gaming experience was a subjective task. To mitigate this, we would like to invite new players to test our game and provide feedback.

To avoid straying from our intended direction, the same group of leaders would also review work-in-progress designs, artwork, and audio treatments in weekly 'show and tell' meetings. Unfortunately, these meetings did not deliver on their intended purpose. The focus shifted from the work itself to critiquing the individuals behind it, leading to a fear of sharing incomplete work. This hindered early course correction opportunities.

Based on the observations from these reviews and meetings, the senior leadership would envision the next desired state of the game. Sometimes, fixed dates were assigned to these targets, although their achievability was not always thoroughly assessed. Another group, including myself, acted as intermediaries between the senior leadership and the talented team members. We would collaborate with craft experts to develop a plan that aligned with the envisioned future state. This plan would then be communicated to the team, setting targets for a four-week milestone. Execution would be closely managed in daily meetings until the milestone's completion, followed by a review before starting the next milestone immediately.

As the complexity of game development increased and teams grew larger, the limitations of our approach and our ability to lead effectively became evident. The challenges became more pronounced.

In his captivating book, "The Antidote: Happiness for People Who Can't Stand Positive Thinking," Oliver Burkeman shares insights from his interview with Chris Kayes, the author of a thought-provoking book on the tragic 1996 Everest disaster. In "Destructive Goal Pursuit," Kayes analyses the mindset and decision-making process that led to the unfortunate deaths of eight climbers on that fateful day. Despite clear evidence suggesting the dangers of their pursuit, they persisted in their goal of reaching the peak of Everest, with fatal consequences.

In *the Antidote, Burkeman says:*

What motivates our investment in goals and planning for the future, much of the time, isn't any sober recognition of the virtues of preparation and looking ahead. Rather, it's something much more emotional: how deeply uncomfortable we are made by feelings of uncertainty. Faced with the anxiety of not knowing what the future holds, we invest ever more fiercely in our preferred vision of that future—not because it will help us achieve it, but because it helps rid us of feelings of uncertainty in the present. "Uncertainty prompts us to idealise the future," Kayes told me. "We tell ourselves that everything will be OK, just as long as I can reach this projection of the future."

There is massive uncertainty in developing a video game project, and the larger the team, the greater the uncertainty. In '*Destructive Goal Pursuit*', Kayes breaks down the characteristics that lead to what he termed goalodicy:

- Pressure to continually achieve higher goals.
- Increased use of rigid outcome performance criteria.
- Greater inter-organisational competition.
- Declining value of long-term relationships with employees.
- Action Orientation.

- Drive towards short-term performance.
- Reliance on short-term projects such as task forces and ad hoc teams to carry out tasks.
- Ability for individual actions to affect team or organisational outcomes.
- Multicultural environment.
- Coordination of work spanning time and space.
- Unpredictable, even hostile environment.
- Placement of personal goals before organisational goals.
- Participants' alienation from organisations.

In our relentless pursuit of innovation and quality in our games, we unintentionally created an environment filled with challenging conditions. Our goals became increasingly short-term, leading to intense pressure and urgency. We formed specialised teams to improve specific aspects of the game, and sub-teams were compared on leaderboards, creating a competitive atmosphere. Individual actions could have a significant impact on the entire team, sometimes resulting in tension. Our team was composed of individuals from various parts of the world, adding to the complexity of communication and collaboration.

Our leadership approach during this time can be best described as an evolved version of the traditional 'command-and-control' method, which I prefer to call 'mask and task'. It required leaders and managers to wear a mask of inauthenticity, pretending to have all the answers and knowing the best way forward. However, in the reality of game development and many other complex endeavours, this approach falls short. Critical decisions were made outside the small group of leaders, but the lack of shared context hindered their effectiveness.

Controlling and executing tasks according to the plan took longer than anticipated, and we lacked the agility to respond quickly to changes in the commercial, creative, and technical landscape. Despite the need for adjustments, we remained rigid in our pursuit of predetermined targets.

Our milestone-driven process failed to account for the need for reflection and adaptation between milestones. We were constantly focused on achieving targets without taking the time to learn and improve. As a result, I felt powerless and incapable of making a difference. It wasn't just about seeking status or a higher position; it was a deep-seated belief that my true leadership potential could only be realised with a specific title.

Anonymous feedback during a 360-degree appraisal confirmed my loss of confidence, a truth that I struggled to accept at the time.

Reflecting on those challenging days, I now realise that I had surrendered my power and succumbed to the belief that my job title defined my worth. The immense stress I experienced was a direct consequence of putting myself under constant pressure to provide command to the team and updates and context to the controlling group. I felt trapped and overwhelmed, unable to escape the self-imposed burdens I carried.

Crash

By 2012, I had progressed in my career and assumed the role of line producer. This position served as a bridge between the creative vision and the production team, allowing me to navigate the process of translating the game's creative direction into actionable priorities for the team. It was my responsibility to ensure that the team's efforts were aligned with the desired outcome.

In this role, I acted as a conduit, conveying the progress and constraints of the production to the creative direction. It involved a delicate balance of understanding the creative goals while also considering the practicalities and limitations of the development process. It was my task to find the middle ground where creativity and practicality could coexist harmoniously.

As a line producer, I had the privilege of working closely with both the creative minds and the talented production team. It was an exhilarating experience to witness the transformation of ideas into tangible progress. The collaborative nature of the role allowed me to bring clarity and focus to the team, ensuring that everyone understood their roles and responsibilities in the grand scheme of the game's development.

While challenges certainly arose along the way, the role of a line producer provided me with a unique perspective and the opportunity to foster effective communication between the creative and production aspects of the project. It was a rewarding position that allowed me to contribute to the overall success of the game while maintaining a deep appreciation for the creative vision that sparked its inception.

Looking back at my time working on Most Wanted, I can't help but acknowledge the immense weight of responsibility that I willingly took upon myself. It seemed like there was an endless stream of tasks and challenges, and I embraced them with unwavering determination.

I felt a deep sense of accountability, not only for the success of the game but also for the well-being of everyone involved. I wanted to ensure that every aspect of the project was running smoothly and that my team members were supported in their work. In my pursuit of perfection, I sometimes forget to consider my own limitations.

But I wasn't alone in shouldering this burden. My fellow game leaders were also grappling with their own set of challenges and pressures. We were all united in our shared goal of creating something extraordinary, but the toll it took on us was evident. We pushed ourselves to the limit, driven by a shared passion for excellence.

In retrospect, I realise that I may have been too consumed by my own drive and determination. I relied heavily on my fellow game leaders, expecting them to bear the same weight of responsibility as I did. It was a collective struggle, and while we supported each other, we were all suffering under the weight of our commitments.

Looking back, I wish I had recognised the importance of balance and self-care. It's essential to acknowledge our own limitations and seek support when needed. As leaders, we must remember that we are not invincible and that relying solely on ourselves can lead to burnout and diminished well-being.

Matt Webster, a good friend and fellow leader, described how he felt about leading at the time:

I felt exhausted and unfulfilled, and I was questioning my purpose. For me, I wanted to make amazing game experiences with a like-minded group of talented people who can make wonderful things, but we just weren't there. It struck me that if we'd carried on as we were, we could have killed someone. And that's not being dramatic; it was poor practice, misguidance, and just things not changing to reflect our changing times. We were loading more and more stress onto people, and it was only going to be a matter of time before that would take someone to some really dark places.

As the project neared the alpha deliverable, the pressure on me reached a breaking point. The alpha stage is a critical milestone in game development, where every feature and type of content should be represented, and the entire game should be testable. It marks the beginning of the final phase before the game's release, usually about three months prior to printing the discs.

During this time, my stress levels skyrocketed to unprecedented heights. It took a toll on my physical and mental well-being. Eating became a struggle, and sleep seemed to elude me. To cope with the overwhelming pressure, I found myself turning to alcohol as a form of self-medication. My nights were filled with restless thoughts, desperately trying to solve work problems in my mind. When sleep did come, it was a fleeting and restless experience, as I would awaken at the crack of dawn with a sense of dread, accompanied by bouts of dry retching and anxiety.

The mornings became a battle as I would pause my car on the way to work, caught in the grips of overwhelming emotions and the weight of the day's challenges. The mere thought of facing the tasks ahead was enough to trigger these physical reactions.

It was a dark and difficult time for me. I now know that this was the point where my limbic system gave up. As Dr Cantopher explains in *Curse of the Strong*:

"Like any other physical system, the limbic system has a limit, and if it is stressed beyond this point, it will break. When this happens, the parts of the system that fail are the transmitter chemicals, serotonin and noradrenaline. These are the chemicals that allow the electrical impulse to pass from the end of one nerve fibre to the beginning of the next. In depressive illness, their levels fall rapidly, resulting in the circuit coming to a grinding halt."

When our brain lacks essential chemicals like serotonin and noradrenaline, it can have a profound impact on our emotional well-being and overall functioning. I was experiencing the effects of this deprivation, feeling a deep sense of numbness and an inability to find joy in the things that would typically bring happiness.

It was as if a veil had been cast over my emotions, dulling the vibrancy of life's experiences. The simple pleasures that once sparked excitement and delight now felt distant and unattainable. It was disheartening to witness the loss of normal functions that I had once taken for granted.

The absence of serotonin and noradrenaline had a far-reaching impact, affecting not only my ability to experience pleasure but also influencing my mood, motivation, and overall sense of well-being. It felt as if I was merely existing, going through the motions without the depth and richness that emotions provide.

This stark realisation served as a reminder of the intricate workings of our brain chemistry and the profound influence it has on our mental and emotional states. It was a humbling experience to witness firsthand the power of these neurotransmitters and the intricate balance they contribute to our daily lives.

What We Resist Persists

When my persistent anxiety overwhelmed me and pushed me into a state of depression, I resisted the idea of being unwell for a long time. I would tell myself things like, "Hey, you're one of those people who are depressed." The truth was, I was indeed experiencing depression.

Being clinically depressed is not simply feeling down or fed up. It goes beyond the normal range of emotions and involves losing the belief that one will ever experience positive emotions again. That was precisely how I felt during that time. Even observing positive emotions in others seemed absurd to me. I vividly recall driving home one evening and hearing Peter Allen engaging in light-hearted banter with a co-presenter on BBC Radio 5 Live's Drive programme. At that moment, I couldn't comprehend how anyone could be happy when the world appeared devoid of joy.

I became profoundly disappointed in myself for lacking optimism, seeing it as a sign of weakness that I wanted to avoid. I believe societal conditioning played a role in shaping this judgement. There is an unwritten rule that men should never be perceived as weak, and this message is ingrained in boys from an early age.

Let's take a moment to reflect without any self-censorship. Finish this sentence: "As a man in our current society, the worst thing to be thought of as is _____ "

What was the first word that came to your mind? In my experience, many women struggle to answer this question, while men often respond with "weak." This societal expectation of male strength and invulnerability is deeply ingrained.

Now, let's consider this question: "As a woman in our current society, the worst thing to be thought of as is _____ "

Again, what was the first word that came to mind? Many men may not have a clear answer, but women can often articulate variations of "unattractive," "fat," "ugly," or "unlikable."

46

It's a terrible burden for all of us to bear. However, for me, there is no doubt. Just look at the imagery and text used in advertising. For example, there is a TV advert for vitamin tablets aimed at men, depicting a seemingly perfect man who wakes up at 5:30 AM, drives his trendy and expensive car to work out, then proceeds to his glamorous job as a model or actor before jetting off to major international cities to sign important business contracts. While this may be an extreme example, it is not isolated or out of touch with prevailing norms.

Like many boys, I grew up knowing that being weak was unacceptable. I also had an intense fear of being alone, losing human connection, and feeling unworthy. This fear fuelled my belief that if I left my job, I would never find another one, despite my education, experience, and past successes.

To avoid vulnerability, which I associated with weakness, I went to great lengths to appear perfect in everything I did. I made an unconscious agreement with myself, believing that if I excelled in every aspect, I would never have to expose my vulnerabilities, yet everyone would still want to connect with me because of my perceived perfection.

However, deep within me, a part of me was searching for something more. I was drawn to Brene Brown's 'Power of Vulnerability' and found myself watching it repeatedly. Brene's story of experiencing a breakdown at the same time she realised the power of vulnerability as a gateway to human connection resonated profoundly with me, bringing tears to my eyes. She emphasised that vulnerability is "the birthplace of joy, of creativity, of belonging, of love." Something deep within me yearned to dismantle my defences and seek help.

Shortly after leaving work, I visited my GP. Despite the voice in my head saying, "You've given up because you're weak. You don't have a medical condition," I mustered the courage to tell my doctor that I believed I was depressed. This revelation didn't surprise him, as he had recently seen me for the results of a colonoscopy to confirm my stress-induced irritable bowel syndrome (IBS). I suspect he recognised the state I was in and sensed that my health anxiety played a significant role. While the colonoscopy offered a way to temporarily escape the pressure, I was putting myself under, my mental state at the time was clearly in need of attention.

During our discussion, my doctor asked me to fill out a questionnaire, a standard diagnostic tool used by the NHS. The questions asked me to consider the past few weeks of my life and rate the symptoms of depression I had experienced. Each question required me to assess the frequency of the symptoms, ranging from 'Not at all' to 'Nearly every day'.

The questionnaire revealed the extent of my struggles:

- Little pleasure or interest in doing things? Every day. All I could think about was work or escaping work.
- Feeling down, depressed, or hopeless? Every. Single. Day.
- Trouble sleeping or sleeping too much? Barely sleeping.
- Feeling tired or lacking energy? Always tired, experiencing caffeine-fuelled highs and crashing lows.
- Poor appetite or overeating? Barely eating.
- Feeling like a failure or letting myself and my family down? Are you kidding? Those thoughts consumed me.
- Trouble concentrating on activities like reading or watching TV? Not really, but only because I engaged in so few leisure activities.
- Moving or speaking slowly, or feeling fidgety? Interestingly, I was hyper-focused on achieving goals, which could be described as "fidgety."
- Thoughts on being better off dead or self-harming? That question caught me off guard, as I hadn't considered it. The answer was "Not at all," the only question I could respond to in that way. The others were 'On more than half the days' or 'Nearly every day'.

Years later, without warning, that moment resurfaced, and I found myself in tears, realising that the line I didn't cross was the only glimmer of light amidst the darkness. I believe many people wanted to ask me that question, but for various reasons, they hesitated. I was convinced I was failing, yet I never regarded myself as a failure. In hindsight, I now recognise the importance of asking that question. It could save someone's life.

Filling out that questionnaire marked the first step in acknowledging that perhaps there was something wrong with my health rather than with me as a person. Strangely, it brought peculiar comfort, as it transformed the problem into a tangible issue that could be addressed. Problem-solving is something I'm familiar with, and now I could apply that skill to my own well-being.

Acceptance

Therapy

I realised how fortunate I was to have private health coverage provided by my employer, which allowed me to receive care from Dr Cantopher. He referred me to an exceptional therapist named Baz, who guided me through a course of cognitive-behavioural therapy (CBT). There are various types of therapy, and much has been written about their effectiveness. From what I've read and personally experienced, the therapeutic relationship between patient and therapist plays a crucial role in fostering positive change. Baz treated many individuals like me who held leadership positions, were driven by achievement, and were excessively focused on goals. He wouldn't let me persist with my negative patterns.

The initial three months were particularly challenging. Some describe individuals battling depression, and during that period, it truly felt like a battle to break free from the spiral of negative thoughts and establish healthier patterns. Being an avid reader, I devoured every book Baz recommended to the point where he had to advise me to take a break and give myself time to process the information. I was trying too hard to be the perfect patient, much like I had strived to be the perfect employee.

A dear friend from work sensed my self-judgement and anxiety about being away, and she reassured me by saying, "Your job right now is to focus on getting well." Her words brought comfort.

Dr Cantopher emphasised, during my first appointment with him, the importance of giving the brain a rest during the recovery process. It wasn't about doing nothing but rather avoiding excessive mental strain. He suggested I watch Australian soap operas, of all things! For me, it became a combination of various activities. I had a deep curiosity about depression that I wanted to satisfy, so I immersed myself in reading on the subject. I searched for movies featuring characters struggling with depression and watched films like 'Sideways' and 'Garden State'. I listened to music created by artists who had experienced depression, with Elgar's 'Nimrod' resonating deeply with me. Poetry also played a significant role in my healing journey. Additionally, I played golf on my own, which allowed me to engage in some physical exercise and connect with nature.

Working with Baz, I began to understand that I had internalised some unconscious beliefs that were undermining me. The most pervasive of these was the belief that "perfect is the minimum standard." This belief was deeply problematic because perfection is an elusive and fleeting moment that rarely occurs. Consequently, I found myself frequently disappointed with myself, leading to the core belief I needed to let go of: "I am not enough."

Now, when I hear someone proudly identify as a perfectionist, it makes me cringe. It's a warning sign for me. Similarly, the phrase 'practice makes perfect' has a similar effect. In reality, practicing flawed techniques only reinforces ineffective approaches. In truth, practice makes it permanent. However, what is more dangerous about that phrase, in my perspective, is the implication that perfection is attainable. That notion now sounds like a distraction from genuine learning and personal development.

Striving for perfection also compelled me to try to be everything to everyone, which, I now recognise, is utterly impossible. Attempting to do so only turns one into a liar.

At work, it meant I carried the belief that I alone should always have all the answers and that it was my duty to constantly tell my team members what to do. I never fully allowed myself to accept the moments when I felt alone and afraid.

Discovering Mindfulness

During my three months away from work and throughout the nine months I continued working with Baz, I delved into mindfulness at his recommendation. Baz pointed me towards Jon Kabat-Zinn, a remarkable medical professor known for bringing mindfulness into the mainstream through his Mindfulness-Based Stress Reduction program. I began my exploration with Kabat-Zinn's book "Wherever You Go, There You Are," which deeply moved me. One particular quote resonated strongly: "We work on ourselves to help others, but we also help others to work on ourselves."

It became clear to me that this was part of my journey. I had always felt a deep connection with game developers, recognising them as my tribe. Attending the Game Developers Conference in San Francisco and being surrounded by passionate, innovative, and diverse individuals confirmed this. I knew I wanted to work on myself to help game developers, and intuitively, it made sense to incorporate mindfulness into my life. Intellectually, I understood that the core concept of non-judgmental observation of thoughts and emotions in mindfulness could be a vital strategy for preventing a relapse into depression. However, I doubted my ability to succeed in practicing mindfulness. I didn't think I had the discipline to stick with it.

Despite my reservations, I made the decision to start, even with the belief that I couldn't succeed. I acquired the book 'Mindfulness: The Eight-Week Meditation Programme for a Frantic World' by Penman and Williams. The book introduced a mindfulness meditation practice for each week, with an introduction preceding the first chapter. I set aside time away from my family each day to engage in the practice. Negative thoughts often arose, whispering things like "You'll never stick to this." I wasn't sure what benefits I would derive from the practice, and I found myself waiting for some breakthrough moment or a significant change in my thoughts. Most of the meditations centred around focusing on the breath, bringing my attention to the exhale and inhale. Frequently, my mind would wander to other thoughts, and the self-critical notion of 'you are bad at meditation' would surface. Some days, I missed the practice, and many times, I contemplated giving up. I couldn't perceive any noticeable benefits. However, in the sixth week, the concept of befriending was introduced.

The befriending meditation became a turning point for me. One aspect of the practice encouraged offering love and kindness to oneself. Initially, I struggled with this, as I still carried a strong sense of self-blame for my suffering. The practice acknowledged this difficulty and suggested an alternative approach:

"If you find it difficult to bring any sense of friendship towards yourself, bring to mind a person or even a pet who loves you or loved you unconditionally. Once you have a clear sense of their love for you, see if you can extend this same love to yourself. May I be safe, happy, and healthy, and may I have ease of being."

This approach started to feel possible. I began to sense the potential to offer myself kindness through the lens of others' love for me. The practice concluded with:

"Finally, extend loving and kindness to all beings, including your loved ones, strangers, and even those whom you find difficult. The intention here is to extend love and friendship to all living beings on the planet, remembering that 'all living beings' include you."

This unlocked something within me. The idea that I was part of a group that I wished well began to reveal how harshly I had treated myself compared to how I tried to treat others. With each repetition of the practice, this concept rooted itself deeper within me. I realised I needed to forgive myself and be kinder.

Gradually, my attitude towards 'failing' at meditation began to shift. Instead of berating myself and giving up whenever I reached the end of a week without fully completing the practice, I found the strength to start again in the same week. I returned to the earlier weeks of the course with a changed mindset. I learned that mindfulness was not about striving towards a goal, which was a departure from most things I had done in my life. The practice wasn't about reaching a destination; it was about experiencing the present moment as it truly was, with minimal judgement. I started to genuinely notice my own thoughts, which was profound for me. Creating a gap between stimulus and response allowed me to recognise the prevalence of negative and self-critical thoughts.

It gave me the opportunity to assess the truth of these thoughts and decide whether I needed to respond or simply let them be. Slowly, I began to apply this awareness even outside of meditation. Although I didn't always succeed in offering myself kindness, I understood its significance and the importance of continuing to practice. I began to view the process of noticing when my attention drifted and intentionally bringing it back as the essence of mindfulness practice—a mental workout akin to lifting weights in the gym for our mental well-being. Each time, I was building the mental resilience necessary to heal and, hopefully, maintain my well-being.

Fun Making Fun

During 2013, while I was back at work and still in therapy, a new opportunity for change emerged. A change in leadership and the unwavering support of EA created a glimmer of hope. Matt took on the role of general manager at Criterion and invited me to join his senior leadership team. Together, we were determined to find a better way of working.

We began by asking a simple yet profound question: "Why isn't it fun to make fun?" We had been immersed in misery for far too long, creating entertainment while feeling completely disconnected from joy. We refused to accept the absurdity of that reality any longer.

Our first step was to follow our instincts and identify the barriers that prevented us from experiencing joy while creating. We sought to remove these obstacles and amplify the factors that enhanced our enjoyment, all while still meeting our goals. Collaboration became a focal point as we recognised the power of working together. We embraced experimentation, allowing ourselves to take risks and explore new possibilities. We dedicated more time to playing games, both our own and those created by others, recognising the importance of experiencing joy firsthand.

Autonomy, Mastery and Purpose

The premise of Daniel Pink's *Drive. The surprising truth about what motivates us* seemed to codify what we instinctively felt:

When it comes to motivation, there is a gap between what science knows and what business does. Our current business operating system, which is built around external, carrot-and-stick rewards, doesn't work and often does harm. We need an upgrade. And science shows the way.

The news system has three essential elements:

i. *Autonomy: the desire to direct our own lives.*
ii. *Mastery: the urge to get better and better at something that matters.*
iii. *Purpose: the yearning to do what we do in the service of something larger than ourselves.*

We started to change how we were working to maximise these three driving factors. We looked at how we could maximise this for our people:

Autonomy as much as possible over the three Ts: Team, Task, and Technique.

Mastery finding work focus that enables people to get better at something they care about.

Purpose for us in the games industry is often the game, but increasingly, finding a healthy, fun way to make fun, a part of our purpose.

RAMP Up

Reading Pink's book and starting to understand the science of motivation was revolutionary for me in my thinking as a leader. I realised that everything I had been trying to do, to help a small group of people control a wider team of talented people, was counterproductive to producing the engaged and motivated team that we needed and wanted. I remembered a comment from that first Burnout retrospective: "Too much micromanagement." People don't want or need that; they need direction and constraints to understand how they succeed. Then they need the autonomy to achieve that success using their unique skills and insights.

I realised there was something missing in the AMP formula, however, and that was recognition. That isn't recognition in the form of a salary or bonus; science tells us they are really hygiene factors when it comes to engagement and motivation. This is really, at its heart, 'Well done' or 'Thank you' from someone you respect. I still believe this is the most powerful form of recognition. I realised I personally craved that and had been starved of it for years, contributing to my declining self-esteem. I resolved that in the teams I lead, people would get the recognition they deserved—not false recognition but genuine respect for what they contributed.

The New Criterion Philosophy

We talked as a leadership group every day at that time about how we wanted to work and how we could improve next. We found that we were able to express our new philosophy towards processes and people in two statements:

- Treat People as Talent.
- No Dogma.

The phrase 'You get what you expect, and you deserve what you tolerate' just kept emerging for me time after time. I searched for the phrase but could never find a definitive source. However, it really made sense for the philosophy that we were distilling from our new way of working: we expect talent and passion, and we will not tolerate dogma.

I documented three key pillars of our No Dogma approach to process: people-driven processes, favoured autonomy, and Goldilocks goals for mastery.

People-driven process: We realised, as we intuitively believed, that process exists to serve people and not the other way around. However, we noticed that we had seen ourselves and other teams dogmatically following their process, regardless of whether it was working for them. I worked with members of the team to define what we believe a useful process is. We came up with this:

- Ask each other the right questions.
- Make better decisions.
- Know what to expect of each other.
- Work as effectively as possible.

To be truly people-driven, the process had to adapt to the people using it as it was executed. This doesn't necessarily mean less process, but rather asking if the process we are using is best serving the people using it, and if it is not, actively changing it.

Within well-aligned priorities and constraints, favour autonomy: Our intention was to maximise our talent's autonomy over team (who they work with), task (what people work on), and technique (how they work on it). This was achieved by aligning at the start of each 7-week cycle on priority, budget, and intention, and then teams self-forming within those constraints. Those teams could then choose the technique that best suited their goals. This is the opposite of a small group of people planning and trying to control the execution by a wider talent base.

Goldilocks goals for mastery: We know from Mihaly Csikszentmihalyi's work that flow is defined as "Optimal experiences when the challenges we face are exquisitely matched to our abilities." The Goldilocks goal could be described as "Beyond what someone knows they can do and short of what they believe is impossible." We work hard to set goals collaboratively to maximise the opportunity for flow at Criterion.

We also distilled 3 key pillars of treating people as talent: Presume passion to build a team; know your team; drop command and control; embrace inspiration and influence.

Presume Passion: As leaders at Criterion, we are not asking anyone to prove that they are passionate about their craft or about the game they are making. This had to be a given, as was the framing for all interactions.

To Build a Team, Know Your Team: We believed that it was important that we get to know each other from the motivational level onwards. This means having powerful conversations about things like:

- Work preference style: some individuals prefer high stimulus, high disruption, and the opposite.
- Thinking style: to what extent is each individual led by their head, heart, and gut?
- Do people prefer to solve project problems through people, products, or processes?

In discussion with Ken, one of our senior engineers, we had a meaningful conversation that led us to define the types of problem spaces that people may find most motivational to work in. We realised that the level of motivation could vary based on how clearly defined the problem and solution were for different challenges. This insight allowed us to develop a shared language for discussing different work styles. It was a collaborative effort that took into account the diverse perspectives and experiences within our team.

	Fuzzy solution	Well defined solution
Well defined problem	**Expert**	**Craft**
Loosey defined problem	**Discovery**	**Connection**

Drop Command and control, embrace, inspire, and coach: We recognised that a command-and-control approach was limiting and did not provide the optimal environment for our talented developers to thrive. As a result, we embraced a different approach rooted in compassion and servant leadership. Our goal was to inspire and coach our team members, empowering them to unleash their full potential and make meaningful contributions. We fully believed that by fostering a culture of inspiration and coaching, we could create a more dynamic and fulfilling work environment for everyone involved.

Ramping Up: Our Seven-week Cycle

We established a rhythm of working that resonated with our philosophy and allowed us to effectively manage our projects. This rhythm consisted of a seven-week cycle, which became our milestone for the project. Let me break down the different stages of this cycle for you:

> ➢ Work Weeks: The majority of the milestone, roughly six weeks, was dedicated to focused work. We divided this period into three two-week sprints, allowing our teams to make significant progress on their assigned tasks.
> ➢ Planning Week: After the work weeks, we dedicated one week to what we called the "Planning Week." This week served multiple purposes:

- Closing the Last Milestone: The first two days of Planning Week were devoted to wrapping up the previous milestone. We reviewed the progress made, evaluated the outcomes, and tied up any loose ends to ensure a smooth transition to the next phase.

- Deliberate Recharging: The following two days were dedicated to deliberate recharging. We recognised the importance of rest and rejuvenation to maintain productivity and well-being. During this time, team members were encouraged to take a break, recharge their energy, and engage in activities that brought them joy and relaxation.
- Reshaping and Replanning: The final day of planning week was focused on reshaping and replanning. We took the opportunity to reflect on the progress made, assess any changes or new insights, and adjust our plans accordingly. This allowed us to adapt and optimise our approach for the upcoming work weeks.

This seven-week cycle provided us with a clear structure and cadence, ensuring that we had dedicated time for focused work, reflection, and rejuvenation. It helped us maintain momentum, align our goals, and continuously improve our processes throughout the project.

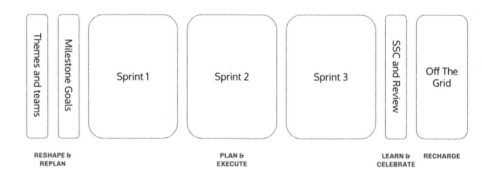

Planning Weekday 1: Learn and Celebrate

During our planning week, specifically on the first day, we implemented a new approach to learning and celebrating our achievements. We noticed that we had been spending more time focusing on what wasn't working well and what we still needed to accomplish, rather than acknowledging and celebrating what had gone right in our work.

To address this imbalance, we divided the day into two distinct activities: a morning retrospective and an afternoon celebration. In the morning, each feature team conducted a retrospective using the 'Start, Stop, Continue' method, allowing them to reflect on their progress, identify areas for improvement, and make actionable plans for the future.

In the afternoon, we gathered as a team for a big sharing session. This was an opportunity for individuals to showcase and celebrate their achievements over the previous six weeks. Anyone who wanted to participate could stand in front of the team and share their work. This created a social contract where individuals felt empowered to be vulnerable, knowing that their accomplishments would be acknowledged and supported by their colleagues. The morning discussions had already addressed any challenges or difficult conversations, making the afternoon celebration feel more natural and uplifting.

To further enhance peer recognition, we introduced a "wall of awesome." Each achievement was written on a note card and stuck to the wall. At the end of the sharing session, every team member had the opportunity to post a sticker on their favourite achievement from each feature team. Additionally, they could choose one special sticker to represent their favourite overall accomplishment. This peer recognition system proved to be incredibly powerful, fostering a sense of appreciation and support among team members.

By dedicating time to both learning and celebration, we created a positive and balanced environment where accomplishments were acknowledged, achievements were shared, and individuals felt valued for their contributions. It not only boosted team morale but also encouraged continuous improvement and a sense of collective pride in our work.

Planning Weekday 2 and 3: Off the Grid

During the second and third days of our planning week, which typically fall on Tuesday and Wednesday, we implemented a unique concept called 'Off the Grid'. These two days were dedicated to providing the team with complete autonomy over their team, tasks, and techniques. The objective was to encourage talent to pursue activities they believed would be highly beneficial but had not planned to do so during the previous six weeks. Importantly, there was no leadership oversight during this time, allowing individuals to explore their own ideas and approaches freely.

The only requirement was that each person had to share their achievements and learnings with at least one other person at the end of the two days. This sharing could take place during the 'Back on the Grid' review session that we organised or in smaller sessions based on individual preferences. Off the Grid became an integral part of our pre-production and early production phases, serving as a valuable opportunity for recharging and learning.

During Off the Grid, team members had the freedom to choose their focus, whether it be working on specific features, exploring new tools and workflows, participating in Game Jams, engaging in board game development, experimenting with new hardware, or even delving into areas beyond their usual scope. For example, our senior engineers took the opportunity to upgrade from Unity 4 to Unity 5, while artists explored techniques such as photo scanning and building dioramas.

The benefits of Off the Grid were numerous and impactful:

- It liberated people's thinking, allowing them to break free from constraints and conventional approaches.
- Individuals became more willing to take creative risks and explore innovative ideas.
- Time constraints of two days trained individuals to deliver within a fixed and focused timeframe.
- People had the chance to experiment with new roles, taking on responsibilities as team leaders or project managers.
- Since Off the Grid did not require active leadership, it provided our regular leaders with valuable reflection space, enabling them to step back and gain fresh perspectives.

Overall, Off the Grid fostered a culture of autonomy, exploration, and continuous learning within our team. It nurtured creativity, encouraged personal growth, and ultimately contributed to the overall success and innovation of our projects.

Planning Weekday 4 and 5: Reshape and Replan

On the fourth and fifth days of our planning week, which typically fall on Thursday and Friday, we engage in the crucial activities of reshaping and replanning. Within a well-aligned context of studio priorities, our team members are given the freedom of choice over their teams, tasks, and techniques.

On Thursday mornings, project and studio leads presented the project context, goals, outcomes, and priority themes. Team members discussed and chose their preferred groups for the next phase, considering both the work and collaborators. The process sparked discussions and deepened understanding.

Once the teams were formed, they would split off and spend time figuring out what they believed they could achieve in the upcoming six weeks. By the end of Thursday, each team would have defined their specific goals and set their sights on what they aimed to accomplish collectively. This process allowed for active participation and ownership in shaping the team's objectives, ensuring that each member felt invested in the outcomes to be achieved.

Reshaping and replanning offered a structured yet flexible approach to aligning our efforts and setting clear objectives for the next phase. It empowered team members to have a voice in determining their work priorities, fostering a sense of autonomy, purpose, and collaboration within the studio.

In order to strike the right balance, we asked ourselves, "What is the maximum amount of autonomy we can afford the team?" We aimed to provide them with as much autonomy as possible while avoiding overwhelming them with choices. During pre-production, when there were fewer dependencies, we allowed for wider autonomy in areas like world design. However, as we entered full production, we found it necessary to tighten restrictions on what needed to be delivered.

We were cautious about offering false autonomy. If there were certain roles or tasks that were non-negotiable, we made that clear upfront to avoid any disillusionment later on. We didn't want to present choices and then backtrack, as that would be demotivating for the team.

To address fewer motivating tasks, we developed the 'Champagne glass tower approach'. This involved prioritising fewer appealing tasks at the top of the pyramid, ensuring they were completed before moving on to more engaging themes. However, we emphasised the importance of psychological safety within the team to encourage open and meaningful discussions.

In practice, we discovered that team members were willing to take on less enjoyable tasks even when it wasn't necessary. To address this, we added the guidance of "No silently taking one for the team," encouraging open communication and ensuring that everyone's contributions were aligned with their own motivation and interests.

Teams had the autonomy to set their own goals for the milestone, which allowed for a sense of ownership and alignment. It was not uncommon for certain themes not to garner team support, but we learned that this often indicated the wisdom of the team surpassing the initial selection process. If a theme was not chosen, it could be due to ineffective presentation, a lack of understanding, or simply not being a strong idea. In such cases, we review and potentially refine the theme through additional design and planning work before considering it again.

Before embarking on a milestone, self-formed teams ensured their viability. This typically involved some negotiation and adjustments to ensure all teams were on track. Instead of focusing solely on the intended work, teams shared their intended goals, allowing everyone to understand the intended benefits to be delivered, even if the specific work required may have differed. This approach promoted clarity and collaboration among the teams.

Autonomy Over Technique

Once viable teams were formed, we embraced a diverse range of approaches and encouraged individuals to leverage their unique talents and problem-solving methods. It was fascinating to observe that the most popular approach tended to be time-boxed, especially in the realm of art, where artists would inquire about the allotted time for a particular task. However, we also discovered a correlation between the preferred working style of a group and the most suitable technique they adopted. It was clear that allowing for flexibility in the approach empowered teams to work in ways that best suited their strengths and preferences.

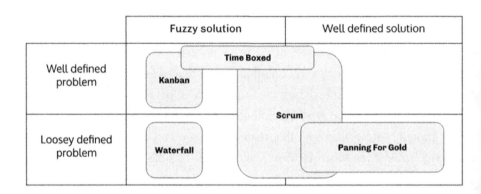

By the end of Friday, our goal was to complete a review of all teams and address any major imbalances in our goals. We would negotiate any necessary adjustments to the team setup to ensure viability and alignment. As the day neared its conclusion, we would embark on a significant desk rearrangement.

Our developer setup, with desks on wheels and simplified connectivity (one power plug and one data plug), facilitated swift and seamless physical restructuring of teams. And to celebrate the week's accomplishments, it was a tradition for everyone to gather at the pub for some well-deserved relaxation and camaraderie.

Mindfulness: From Personal to Team

The potential benefits of mindfulness practice at work resonated with others at Criterion and became a team endeavour. We decided to run an 8-week, 16-hour course to introduce mindfulness to the studio.

The author recommended by my therapist, Baz, was Professor Jon Kabat-Zinn. Kabat-Zinn, a medical professor who studied with Zen Buddhist teachers, brought mindfulness to the West through his Stress Reduction Clinic at the University of Massachusetts Medical School. His programme, known as Mindfulness-Based Stress Reduction (MBSR), gained popularity due to its scientific grounding and the removal of its connection to Buddhism.

I started with Kabat-Zinn's book "Wherever You Go, There You Are," listening to the audiobook during my commute. His narration had a significant impact on me, and one statement stood out: "We work on ourselves in order to help others, but we also help others in order to work on ourselves." This resonated deeply with me, as I learned valuable lessons from managing and coaching others, and I believed many at our studio would benefit from learning mindfulness.

The business case for mindfulness in organisations was presented by Chade-Meng Tan, Google's "Jolly Good Fellow," in his book "Search Inside Yourself." Tan, a former software engineer, developed mindfulness training at Google and co-founded the nonprofit 'Search Inside Yourself Leadership Institute' to offer it to a broader audience. The case he makes is straightforward: mindfulness develops emotional intelligence, which is a key differentiator between great and good employees, and mindfulness is trainable.

Supported by EA, I reached out to a local meditation centre and connected with two teachers, Neil and Sarah. It turned out to be a fortunate call, as Sarah became an excellent coach not only for me but also for many at Criterion. Finding a course leader who shared our company values and possessed training in both business coaching and mindfulness teaching proved essential but challenging.

We started with a 2-hour introduction session led by Sarah, which covered various mindfulness practices and exercises. Almost everyone in the studio attended, and a subsequent survey revealed that the majority expressed interest in exploring mindfulness further.

The 2-hour introduction covered these topics:

1. First guided practice: where is your attention?
2. Mindful walking.
3. Mindfulness of chocolate.
4. Reaction to a stressful experience.
5. Tea Practice.
6. Body Scan.
7. Group sharing.
8. Mindful communication.

Sarah then collaborated with us to develop an 8-week, 16-hour course based on Kabat-Zinn's MBSR and Breathworks Mindfulness for Stress (MfS), tailored to suit the demographics and needs of Criterion. We offered the course to everyone, and fourteen individuals, primarily in leadership positions, opted in.

The goals we set for the course were to equip attendees with tools to manage stress and challenges, monitor their well-being, cultivate self-awareness, improve interpersonal relationships, and enhance empowerment and resilience.

The course was a resounding success. The group approached it with open-mindedness and a willingness to share personal experiences. It was a powerful experience for me to embark on this journey together with others. The value of group practice, as expressed in *Mindfulness: A Practical Guide to Finding Peace in a Frantic World* by co-author Danny Penman, became evident:

"Companionship on the journey will help enormously. When someone encounters a 'block,' having others offer help and support (reminding them that they cannot 'fail' at meditation) is immensely reassuring. Discussing individual experiences also deepens everyone else's experiences. Mindfulness is a journey, and it's great to have companions to share the experience."

In the post-course survey, participants shared powerful testimonies of personal change and also acknowledged the positive impact on their work. The majority reported implementing mindfulness techniques in their daily routines and experiencing greater calm, focus, and improved interactions.

Here are some examples:

- "You can waste too much time thinking and worrying about things that aren't real."
- "Helps me bring awareness and settle my mind."
- "Slowing things down, one thing at a time."
- "Treating myself with compassion."
- "Focusing and capturing positive and happy moments."
- "Makes me think before I say/do something."
- "Remaining grounded when having conversations (listening or speaking)"
- "Being self-aware and having thoughts and emotions is just something that happen to you, not part of you."

These are powerful testimonies of personal change, but we also asked if it was helping people in the workplace, so we asked, "Are you doing anything differently in the way you work as a result of what you've learned on the programme?" We could see there were benefits that were worth further investment:

- "I am trying not to overthink things too much."
- "Taking more breaks, using the STOP practice, and making sure I take some time to enjoy things and be present."
- "Not drastically, but I am doing many of the 'one small thing' practices, such as stopping and letting the good in."
- "Being calmer, less stressed and so able to free up more of my energy for actual work."
- "Yes, I tried to focus on the moment whenever I'm stressed, and I imagined a little exercise with music that I do once in a while."
- "Absolutely. Conversations and interactions are all different. I also listen to things in a very different way."
- "Focus on one thing at a time (and do it slowly)."
- "At the risk of sounding dramatic, I don't think any day will ever be the same again. Thank you for this opportunity."

Everyone expressed their willingness to recommend the course to colleagues, emphasising the importance of individual engagement. We subsequently ran the course with a second group, and as attendees shared their positive experiences, the majority of people in the company eventually participated in the course.

Mindfulness had transitioned from personal practice to a team endeavour, benefiting individuals and enhancing collective well-being at Criterion.

Who Am I?

For me personally, it was a highly formative experience when Sarah introduced us to open-awareness meditation. Unlike the focused attention meditation I had practiced before, open-awareness meditation involved remaining non-judgmentally aware of all experiences as they unfolded. During the first switch from focused to open awareness, I felt a profound shift within myself.

As a teenager, I was captivated by Douglas Adams' 'Hitchhiker's Guide to the Galaxy' series. In one scene, the character Zaphod Beeblebrox is exposed to the 'Total Perspective Vortex', a machine designed to show the vastness of the universe. While others were driven to madness by the realisation of their insignificance, Zaphod emerged invigorated, believing himself to be the most important person in the universe.

My experience with open awareness was reminiscent of Zaphod's encounter with the vortex. I began to perceive myself as part of an infinite universe, distinct from my thoughts and emotions. The revelation was invigorating rather than overwhelming. I realised that I could observe my thoughts and emotions without being consumed by them. This led me to question my identity, asking, "If I am not my thoughts and emotions, who am I?"

In the following months, I delved deeper into this inquiry through continued practice. Drawing from Zen teachings, I embraced the notion that "I am the awareness through which my thoughts and emotions pass." This acknowledgement was a game-changer for me. Although I still found myself occasionally getting caught up in my thoughts and emotions, the experience of being aware and reconnecting with that state brought greater ease and harmony to my life.

The Empathy Trap

Developing Myself—Peeling the Anxiety Onion

For three years, we witnessed the remarkable benefits of our new philosophy in action and the power of our seven-week rhythm. Our team was incredibly engaged, showcasing their ability to create amazing and innovative work. The energy and potency within our studio were palpable, evident to both visitors and those who chose to work with us. People would remark, "This feels like a place where people make games!" The positive atmosphere attracted senior individuals who sought a space where they could be their best selves, even for potentially challenging negotiations.

Throughout this journey, my mindfulness practice played a significant role in managing my anxiety. A pivotal moment was when I learned to deliberately observe my thoughts, realising that the mind is a 'thought-producing organ' rather than the sole definition of my identity. This newfound awareness allowed me to choose my responses instead of simply reacting to every thought. I extended this understanding to my emotions as well, recognising that they too can be observed without necessarily needing an immediate reaction. This shift brought immense release as I differentiated between being identified with my emotions ('I am anxious') and simply observing them ('I am experiencing anxiety') or even more powerfully, acknowledging their presence without personal attachment.

However, by late 2016, a problem emerged. I wasn't unwell, but I also wasn't truly okay. Sleep became a persistent challenge, despite years of working on my anxiety through cognitive-behavioural therapy. Waking up early and struggling to fall back asleep became a regular occurrence. The weight of responsibility I placed on myself, not only for the studio's success but also for the well-being of each individual within it, persisted. Anxiety still haunted me, focusing on my fear of not being able to handle the demands of leadership, both physically and mentally. There was an underlying sense of never being able to offer or give enough, stemming from a personal scarcity mindset. The truth was, I was performing well in my role, and the studio's turnaround was gaining recognition. Yet anxiety disregards facts and operates on its own terms.

Embarking on a Deeper Practice and Recognising Patterns

Recognising the need to address the underlying causes of my anxiety, I realised that I had to confront a problem with my approach to mindfulness practice. Although the essence of mindfulness is not about striving for or achieving a specific outcome, I discovered that I had been treating it as a means to progress or as a solution to a problem. My practice was initially developed as a way to overcome depression and focus on problem-solving. I realised that I had framed it around defending against threats rather than allowing for personal growth and unfolding. Paradoxically, my pursuit of achievement was limiting my true progress.

I observed a distinct cycle I had created, alternating between two phases. Following a period of accomplishment, I would enter an *elevated phase* characterised by a strong sense of ease, openness, and creativity. During this phase, my relationships flourished, and I felt genuinely connected to others. I exuded warmth and approached interactions with a sense of curiosity. However, this elevated state was not sustainable, and it would eventually transition into a *judgmental phase*. In this phase, I became self-critical and judgmental towards both me and others. My expectations would become unreasonably high, triggering anxiety. I would take any perceived lack of performance or dissatisfaction within the team personally.

I became addicted to this pattern of thinking as a means of self-management and sought external recognition to validate my worth. This shift to limbic hijack mode, where the primal part of our mind takes control, was deeply unpleasant. It manifested as tension, headaches, an increased heart rate, shallow breathing, and a narrowed perspective.

It became evident that I was not skilfully managing the threat I felt during these judgmental phases. My coping mechanism was to numb my mind and emotions through various activities. I realised that these numbing activities spanned a wide range, including eating, working, gaming, exercising, and engaging in other distractions that occupied my thoughts and emotions. There was a spectrum of relationships to these activities, ranging from occasional indulgence to dangerous addiction, with a healthy balance being the ideal state.

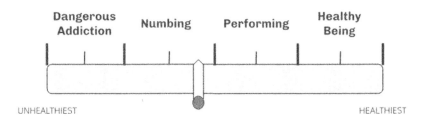

As I reflected on my numbing activities, I celebrated the awareness I had gained. I noticed that I was constantly shifting between activities, playing a game of 'whack-a-mole' as one numbing behaviour replaced another. It was clear that I couldn't sustain this cycle indefinitely. I yearned for a more peaceful inner life and recognised the need for a breakthrough in this pattern.

Embracing Transformation and Cultivating Peace

As my desire to accelerate my personal growth and self-understanding grew stronger, I faced the challenge of letting go. Despite my efforts, I still struggled with poor sleep and yearned for freedom from the burdens I had allowed to oppress me. However, I also clung to the self-image I had constructed around these burdens. I carried a heavy sense of responsibility for others and often found myself waiting for permission, both from myself and from external triggers, to initiate change. Questions like "if not now, then when?" frequently surfaced during my practice, challenging me to embrace vulnerability and embrace the opportunity for growth.

Continuing with my meditation practice, one guided session posed a profound question that lingered in my thoughts for days and continues to resurface from time to time: "Are you prepared to give up who you think you should be to become the person you really could be?" This question invited deep reflection and prompted me to reassess my beliefs and self-perceptions.

I intentionally worked on cultivating peace in my daily life. I incorporated a personal peace meditation into my daily routine and actively acknowledged moments of peace that naturally arose throughout the day. Gradually, I began to experience positive shifts. I felt a greater sense of calm and clarity, and catastrophising thoughts decreased significantly. I became more open to accepting compliments and acknowledgments from others in a healthy manner. And amidst it all, glimmers of joy emerged, illuminating my journey.

However, disrupted sleep remained a lingering issue, a signal that I still had inner work to do.

My attitude towards my practice and its purpose underwent a transformation. I had previously viewed it as a means to an end, a finite destination. Yet, I realised that I wanted mindfulness to be an integral part of who I am, woven into the fabric of my life's journey. It became less about something I do and more about something I embody.

The Empathy Trap

While we enjoyed the excitement of creating a fun and vibrant working environment, there were underlying challenges that I was facing. Despite the recognition we received when we won the Best Place to Work award in 2017, we were still grappling with our own personal struggles. The team was thriving and finding joy in their work, but it was coming at a high cost for the studio's leadership team.

Our leadership style was built on collaboration and empathy, deeply understanding, and meeting the needs of those we led. However, I began to notice signs of burnout in some members of the leadership team. They were dedicating so much of themselves to empathising with the team and fulfilling their needs that they were neglecting their own well-being. This phenomenon, known as empathic distress, was described by Singer and Klimecki as *a strong aversive response to others' suffering, coupled with a desire to withdraw from the situation to protect oneself from overwhelming negative emotions.*

We realised that we needed to learn and adapt quickly. Going back to a command-and-control style of leadership was not an option; nobody wanted that, and we had already proven to ourselves that it was ineffective. Some leaders took a step back, and together we embarked on a journey to break free from the constraints we had encountered. We recognised the value of our empathetic approach, but we needed to find a way to make it work on a larger scale without sacrificing our own well-being.

Part 2
Liberation

Liberated Leadership
The New Change Cycle

The highest type of ruler is one of whose existence.
the people are barely aware.
Next comes one whom they love and praise.
Next comes one whom they fear.
Next comes one whom they despise and defy.

Tao Te Ching attributed to Lao Tzu.

Developing Myself to Develop Others

As I continued my journey of self-discovery with Sarah's guidance, I found that during my meditative practice, certain experiences required a process of feeling rather than thinking. It became clear to me that our awareness goes beyond our thoughts, and accessing its entirety necessitates a different approach. This process involved allowing things to emerge rather than trying to control or analyse them with the mind. It required a deliberate choice to let go of habitual thinking patterns and create space for a more intuitive and experiential process.

During these practices, a phrase that repeatedly emerged was "as above, so below." Although it surfaced through feeling rather than intellectual analysis, I felt compelled to explore its meaning. I discovered that this phrase originated in Hermeticism and conveyed the concept that the microcosm (the self) and the macrocosm (the universe) are interconnected. This understanding resonated with me, especially in the context of leadership. I realised that organisations reflect the qualities of their leaders, and by working on ourselves, we can positively influence our teams and the entire organisation. I now firmly believe that inner work is an essential component of leadership development rather than an optional add-on.

To Lead is to Serve

As my journey of self-discovery continued, I experienced numerous revelations and accompanying questions. One significant revelation was connected with my life purpose. During a powerful session, a phrase emerged that instantly resonated with me: "to share truth from the heart and to honour others' heartfelt truth." This purpose felt simple yet profound, providing both direction and alignment for how I wanted to lead and relate to others.

I realised that my leadership approach was closely aligned with my broader philosophy of engaging with people and their struggles. It wasn't something separate, but an integral part of who I am. I recognise the different mindsets we can adopt when relating to others, ranging from a victim mindset to a compassionate mindset. Leading from a victim mindset, characterised by feelings of powerlessness, and seeing everything as broken, was ineffective and counterproductive. Developing self-awareness through mindfulness practice helped me recognise when I slipped into a victim mindset and take deliberate steps to address my physical and emotional needs before resuming my leadership role.

Importantly, with the benefit of hindsight, I realised that our emphasis on collaborative leadership had led us into the empathy trap. However, my journey was leading me towards servant leadership grounded in compassion, which aligned with the work of Singer and Klimecki. Their research showed that compassion can serve as a regulation for excessive empathy that leads to empathic distress. Through mindfulness meditation and compassion training, a person's capacity for compassion can be developed.

Fear of Letting Go

When people hear the term "servant leadership," they may mistakenly perceive it as passive or giving away power. I, too, had concerns about this initially. However, I came to understand that it meant stepping fully into our power as leaders. While fundamental aspects such as purpose, commitment, driving change, and passion remained unchanged, it was the mindset and style of leadership that evolved.

When it comes to fear, we have three broad approaches: denial, tolerance, and acceptance.

- Denial: Pretending that we are not afraid, resisting the fear, and avoiding its presence. However, what we resist persists, and denying fear only allows it to persist in the background.
- Tolerance: Resigning ourselves to the existence of fear without actively seeking to change it. It involves recognising fear but feeling powerless to overcome it.
- Acceptance: Embracing the reality of our fear, acknowledging its presence, and understanding the process that creates it. Acceptance allows us to work with fear rather than against it.

While tolerance may precede acceptance, denial is an ineffective strategy. By cultivating acceptance and working on our tolerance, we can navigate fear more skilfully.

The Journey of Cutting the Lesedi La Rona Diamond

The recent acquisition of the Lesedi La Rona, the largest rough diamond in existence, by Lucara Diamond Corp. caught my attention. The responsibility of cutting such a valuable and irreplaceable gem intrigued me. I came across an interview with the jeweller entrusted with this task, and his philosophy resonated deeply with me. When asked about his approach to cutting the diamond, he simply replied, "It will show us how it should be cut." This statement perfectly encapsulated my perspective on tackling big projects. Initially, they may appear as daunting challenges with boundless opportunities, but often the path forward is not immediately clear. However, I firmly believe that if we approach these endeavours with attentive awareness and positive intention, the way forward will reveal itself.

This concept aligns with the principles of Taoism, particularly the notion of Wu Wei, which can be translated as "non-doing." It refers to natural action, where our efforts are effortless and in harmony with the flow of life. In Chinese culture, Wu Wei also signifies cultivating a mental state in which our actions naturally align with the rhythm of life. Today, I strive to approach leadership with this mindset. I feel a strong resonance between this philosophy and the process of developing complex projects. By humbly paying attention and quieting our egos, the way through a complex and chaotic project will unfold before us. It is essential to avoid excessive interference and instead allow the natural order and flow of progress to guide us.

My role as a leader is to facilitate the collaborative discovery of the way. It still involves creating meaningful and transformative change, but it is no longer about forcing outcomes. Instead, it requires a new way of leading that embraces freedom. This newfound freedom liberates me from the anxiety that stemmed from acting outside of authenticity and integrity.

All of this comes together in the Liberated Leadership change cycle.

Pillar #1 Focus on Now

Key Practice: Be present; focus on what you need to do right now.

The secret is here in the present. If you pay attention to the present, you can improve upon it. And, if you improve on the present, what comes later will also be better.

Paulo Coelho, The Alchemist.

What does it truly mean to be present? I believe true presence is exemplified by someone in a life-or-death situation where every moment is fully absorbed. Being present means experiencing joy, lightness, and ease in the present moment. It's not always about changing what we're doing, but rather how we approach it. We must not let the destination overshadow the importance of each step along the way. Challenges are not problems but rather situations that can be addressed or, sometimes, left alone until the right time comes.

Eckhart Tolle's book, "The Power of Now," beautifully delves into the essence of presence. Mindful meditation, a simple form of meditation, involves non-judgmentally directing our attention to the present moment, free from identification with our judgments. This practice serves as the foundation of our presence. In the realm of leadership, being present means focusing on what needs to be done right now.

Our addiction to external stimuli is a prevalent issue in our always-connected world. Researchers from the University of Virginia and Harvard University conducted experiments in which subjects were placed in a room with no distractions except a device that delivered mild electric shocks. Surprisingly, many participants preferred administering electric shocks to themselves rather than being left alone with their thoughts. This experiment underscores the importance of deliberately setting aside time for reflection and cultivating presence, especially in a world filled with constant external stimuli. Establishing a regular mindfulness meditation practice greatly aided me in both recognising when I am not present and reconnecting with the present moment.

The value of presence extends beyond personal development; it also serves as a powerful tool for project management. Embracing the present allows us to let go of assumptions and fears about the future. Sometimes, we can become overwhelmed by the magnitude of the overall project, thinking, "I can't do this now because I'll have to do even more later." However, the truth is that we don't know what will be required until we embark on the journey. We are at our best when fully present, focusing on the next highest priority increment. Moreover, practicing presence in project management enables us to discern what tasks are unnecessary, and as a brilliant graphics engineer once told me, "Doing nothing is the ultimate optimisation."

Being present and embodying my presence is, in my opinion, a service to the team I lead. Although intangible, it creates a calm space that fosters effective and collaborative decision-making. When we plan with presence, we acknowledge that attempting to plan an entire creative project from start to finish is inauthentic because we cannot predict the future with certainty. Yet, completely abandoning planning also fails to serve our team. Thus, we recognised the need for a continuously improving project management process that scales with people, technology, and best practices while aligning with Criterion's values and commitment to servant leadership.

We adopted the Scaled Agile Framework (SAFE) as the foundation for our approach, realising that we didn't have to reinvent the planning framework. What we brought to the table was our unique mindset, infusing it with our values to create an approach that served our teams. This allowed us to compassionately review vulnerability instead of seeking certainty when discussing our plans. Our favourite phrase when presenting plans became, "This is the best wrong we have today," acknowledging that plans are not set in stone but are subject to continuous learning and improvement.

Key Points

- To be present means fully immersing oneself in the current moment and experiencing joy, lightness, and ease. It's about how we approach tasks, rather than simply changing what we do.

- We need to deliberately set aside time for reflection and cultivate our presence. Regular mindfulness meditation practice aids in recognising and reconnecting with the present moment.
- Presence is not limited to personal development; it is also a valuable tool in project management. Embracing the present allows us to let go of future assumptions and fears.
- Being present benefits the team by creating a calm space for effective and collaborative decision-making.

Pillar #2 Inspire Belief

Key Practice: Quieten your ego and listen with your heart.

The phrase 'Park your ego at the door' or 'No ego here' is often used to emphasise the importance of setting aside our ego when engaging in certain activities. However, it's essential to understand that having an ego is a natural and necessary part of being human. The key is not to deny or pretend that we don't have egoistic needs, but rather to accept and listen to our ego without identifying with it. When we start identifying with our ego and believe that it defines who we are, our egoic needs can dominate our actions and emotional state.

For leaders, allowing personal priorities to dominate projects can lead to reactive and volatile environments where objective reviews of work become overshadowed by desired outcomes. I've experienced such projects, and they tend to be less effective and healthy. To avoid this, it's crucial to develop a quiet ego—one that doesn't seek to control or impose personal priorities on the team being led. Through regular mindful practice, we can free ourselves from attaching our identity to the ego and allow ourselves and those we lead to pursue our dreams.

One of the practices I find powerful for building healthy relationships is taking full ownership of the events in our lives. Recognising that we are the co-creators of our experiences allows us to escape the victim mindset and embrace personal responsibility. Instead of asking, "Why or how has this been done to me?" we can ask, "What actions have I personally taken to lead to this moment?" This perspective empowers us and encourages a proactive approach to our lives.

When people talk, they listen completely. Most people never listen.

Ernest Hemingway.

Mindful listening is another crucial aspect of leading with a quiet ego. When people speak, we must listen fully, without judgement, and with undivided attention. I learned the practice of mindful listening during Google's 'Search Inside Yourself' course, where I discovered its remarkable impact. It involves shifting our focus from observing our own thoughts and emotions non-judgmentally to extending that same mindfulness to another person. Mindful listening fosters deep connections and enriches both the listener and the speaker.

Leading like water, as if flowing around the team we serve, embodies the principles of servant leadership. It entails finding out what the team needs and striving to fulfil those needs. However, it doesn't mean that everyone's problem becomes our own. Instead, it requires using emotional intelligence to discern what the team truly needs, even when it might not align with their immediate wants. This understanding allows us to provide compassionate feedback and support their growth.

Quiet ego doesn't imply self-neglect. On the contrary, it necessitates a massive amount of self-compassion as we make daily judgements about what the team needs. It's essential to watch out for imposter syndrome, a feeling that we don't deserve our success and that we will eventually be exposed as frauds. Imposter syndrome is prevalent among high achievers. A study published in 2011 in the International Journal of Behavioural Science found that an estimated 70 percent of people experience imposter syndrome at some point in their lives. It can lead to overworking, undermining our own success, and worrying excessively about what others think of us. To counteract imposter syndrome, we need to gather actual evidence of cause and effect between performance and outcomes.

As leaders, we can model clear and specific recognition of good performance, providing individuals with the evidence they need to combat imposter syndrome. It's worth noting that we often overestimate how much attention others pay to us. In an experiment, researchers found that people tend to overestimate the amount of attention others give to their actions or appearance.

Researchers assembled groups of students to complete a task in the same room (they were unaware of the true purpose of the experiment). One student was randomly selected as a subject to wear a t-shirt during the activity that would be considered embarrassing. One of the reasons I love this experiment is that it was a Barry Manilow t-shirt that the researchers had gone to the trouble of researching was highly embarrassing for this college population. The researchers

81

asked the subjects wearing the Maniow t-shirt to estimate the percentage of people in the group who would be able to identify the person on the t-shirt at the end of the activity. The subject students estimated it would be around 50 percent, whereas in reality it was only 25 percent.

To back up the personal nature of this, which was judging attention paid to us that was at stake here, researchers also asked other students to watch recordings of these experiments, and they estimated the Manilow-recognition percentage at an accurate 25 percent. So, we overestimate by about 25% how much attention others are paying to us.

This realisation can alleviate unnecessary worry about what others think of us. Moreover, the Dunning-Kruger effect highlights our cognitive bias, where we tend to overestimate our ability in areas where we lack expertise and underestimate our ability in areas where we excel. Embracing a quiet ego means practicing self-compassion, being open to learning, and recognising our limitations.

In essence, leading with a quiet ego requires humility, self-compassion, and a commitment to serving others. It involves letting go of the need to control and impose personal priorities and instead actively listening, learning, and responding to the true needs of the team. By embodying a quiet ego, we create a space where effective and compassionate leadership can thrive.

With a quiet ego, our focus shifts from ourselves to the mission we're working towards and the people we lead who are integral to its success. It allows us to inspire others, instilling in them a belief in our shared mission and, more importantly, a belief in themselves. One of the greatest gifts we can give someone is to genuinely believe in them, especially when they may be grappling with self-doubt.

When we lead with a quiet ego, we create an environment where our mission takes centre stage. It becomes a collective endeavour rather than a personal pursuit. We inspire others by demonstrating our unwavering belief in the mission's value and the potential of those involved. Through our actions and words, we convey the message that each individual's contributions are essential and that they have the power to make a difference.

By believing in others, we provide them with a sense of validation and support. We recognise their strengths, acknowledge their efforts, and encourage their growth. This belief can be particularly powerful for those who may be struggling with self-belief or facing challenges. When they see our genuine faith in them, it can ignite a spark of confidence and resilience within them. It empowers them to tap into their full potential, even when faced with adversity.

Leaders with a quiet ego understand that their role is not to seek personal glory but to uplift others and propel the mission forward. They create a culture of trust, collaboration, and shared purpose. By believing in the capabilities of their team members, they foster an environment where everyone feels valued, motivated, and empowered to bring their best to the table.

In essence, leading with a quiet ego is about shifting the focus from our own egoic needs to the collective aspirations and growth of the team. It's about recognising the power of belief and using it as a catalyst to inspire and empower others. When we genuinely believe in those we lead, we create a ripple effect of confidence, dedication, and success throughout the entire organisation.

Key Points

- To lead with a quiet ego means setting aside your ego and personal priorities when engaging in activities. It doesn't mean denying our egoistic needs, but rather accepting and listening to them without identifying with them.
- Mindful listening, where we fully listen to others without judgement, fosters deep connections.
- Practising self-compassion counters imposter syndrome and cognitive biases. Leading with a quiet ego requires humility, self-compassion, active listening, and responding to the true needs of the team.
- Leaders with a quiet ego uplift others, create a culture of trust and shared purpose, and foster an environment where everyone feels valued and empowered.
- Leading with a quiet ego means shifting the focus from personal needs to the collective aspirations of the team. It involves the power of belief to inspire and empower others, creating a ripple effect of confidence and success throughout the organisation.

Pillar #3 Inspire Trust

Key Practice: Patience with yourself and others.

Yield and overcome;
Bend and be straight;
Empty and be full;
Wear out and be new;
Have little and gain;
Have much and be confused.

Therefore, wise men embrace the one.
And set an example for all.
Not putting on a display, they shine forth. Not justifying themselves, they are distinguished.
Not boasting,
They receive recognition.
Not bragging,
They never falter.
They do not quarrel,
So, no one quarrels with them.
Therefore, the ancients say, "Yield and overcome." Is that an empty saying?
Be really whole,
And evil things will come to you.

Tao Te Ching-attributed to Lao Tzu.

Patience is more than just a virtue; it is a fundamental practice that empowers us to develop trust in all directions. It goes beyond being tolerant or simply waiting for something to happen. Patience is about creating an environment where growth, understanding, and meaningful connections can flourish.

When we exercise patience with ourselves, we extend self-compassion. We acknowledge that personal transformation is a journey that takes time. Instead of rushing to fix everything and becoming overwhelmed, we embrace the mantra, "Be more, do less." We recognise that our presence and authenticity have a greater impact on our leadership than our specific actions. By being patient with ourselves, we allow personal growth to unfold at its own pace, nurturing our own development and well-being.

Equally important is exercising patience with others. As we cultivate patience within ourselves, it naturally extends to those we lead. This involves believing in their potential and offering support as they navigate their own paths. In times when individuals may struggle to believe in themselves, our patient guidance and encouragement can ignite their confidence and inspire them to reach their full potential. Patience becomes a gift we bestow upon them, fostering trust and creating an environment where everyone can thrive.

Patience also plays a vital role in communication.

We must be aware of the ego noise that can hinder effective understanding and connection. Patiently repeating our message multiple times becomes necessary, allowing it to be absorbed amidst competing information. Research suggests that the 'magic number' of repetitions is around seven plus or minus two. By persistently communicating our message until we hear it being reflected back to us, we ensure that it has been truly internalised.

To further enhance the effectiveness of our communication, personalisation is key. Tailoring our message to individuals and considering their unique perspectives makes it more relatable and engaging. By valuing their input and sharing proposals and ideas in a personalised manner, we foster a deeper connection and demonstrate our genuine interest. I have personally experienced the power of personalisation in communication, seeing a significant increase in response rates when adapting my approach to send individual, personal emails to managers.

In summary, patience is a transformative practice that empowers us to lead with freedom and compassion. By cultivating patience with ourselves, others, and in our communication, we create an environment that nurtures growth, understanding, and collaboration. Patience allows us to navigate challenges, build strong relationships, and make a positive impact as leaders. It is through patience that trust blossoms, and together, we can achieve extraordinary outcomes.

Key Points

- Patience is a fundamental practice that fosters trust, creates an environment for growth, and meaningful connections. It involves extending self-compassion and embracing personal transformation as a journey.
- Being patient with others means believing in their potential and offering support.
- Patience in communication involves persistently repeating messages and personalising them for better understanding and engagement.
- Patience empowers us to lead with freedom and compassion, navigating challenges, building relationships, and achieving extraordinary outcomes.

Pillar #4 Ambition in the Mastery Zone

Key Practice: Manage the outcome, not the output.

Agree on Goals Collaboratively

When I was getting ill often, in the stillness of the night, my mind awakened me from a deep slumber, consumed by anxious thoughts. It had become a common occurrence, with my restless mind haunting me during the darkest hours. Desperate for relief, I kept a notebook by my bedside, hoping that by capturing my thoughts on paper, I could release them from the clutches of my racing mind and find solace in sleep once again.

The notebook became my refuge, a safe space to pour out my tangled emotions and overwhelming fears. Each time I woke in the grips of anxiety, I would reach for it, allowing the pen to dance across the pages, giving form to the chaos within. There was something cathartic about transferring those thoughts from the confines of my mind onto the paper, as if by doing so, I could loosen their grip on my weary soul.

Some nights, this ritual worked like magic. The act of writing, of externalising my inner turmoil, would bring a sense of relief and tranquillity. I could feel the weight of my worries gradually dissipate, as if the ink on the page absorbed my fears and transformed them into something tangible, something I could hold and observe from a distance.

But there were nights when the notebook offered no respite, when the words spilled onto the paper yet failed to alleviate the restlessness within me. Those were the nights when my deteriorating mental health cast its shadow most prominently. As my anxious thoughts persisted, they escalated, gripping me in their suffocating embrace. The notebook, once my trusted ally, seemed powerless against the overwhelming darkness that engulfed me.

Amidst the turmoil, a night came unlike any other. I awoke from a dream, its vivid imagery imprinted upon my mind. Something urged me to write it down, not in mere fragments but in great detail. The dream held profound significance—an elusive message yearning to be deciphered. It felt as if my subconscious was desperately trying to communicate, to reveal a truth buried deep within.

This is the scene I dreamt of.

ROB

Hello!

JANE

Hello!

[pause]

I just finished putting up that fence you asked for in the west.

Field.

ROB

That's good. How does it look?

JANE

Great. I had enough of my favourite wood for the entire perimeter. Looks great.

You will definitely love it.

ROB

Oh, dear!

JANE

[Thinks for a moment.]

I thought you wanted me to put up a fence.

ROB

I did…but the fence has to divide West Field in half.

JANE

Right, I'll need some more of my favourite wood?

[Running off]

I love wooden fences.

ROB

No, it needs to be barbed wire.

JANE

Ah…so the goal is we have a barbed wire fence in the West Field.

that divides the field in half. "That sounds good, I'll get straight on it…"

ROB

It has to be done by Friday.

JANE

Oh yeah? [pause] Why's that?

ROB

I have some wolves coming on Friday.

JANE

[incredulous] Wolves?

ROB

Yeah, wolves, like in Dancing with Wolves…not that I'm a Costner fan, although I did like JFK and I'm fond of Field of Dreams.

JANE

Really?

ROB

Yeah, top movies.

JANE

No, I mean, do you really have some wolves arriving on Friday?

ROB

Oh yes, that's why I need the fence.
I want to keep them separate from the sheep in the west field. *[pause]* Or they'll eat them.

JANE

OK, well, there's a bunch of other work to do to make half of that field secure for wolves. I'll run off and get more men. *[He starts to run off.]*

ROB

Wait! *(Bob returns)* What do you think your goal is now?

JANE

Well, I suppose it's 'Keep the wolves away from the sheep in the west field'
Hang on! Why don't we just put them in the East field? It's already.
secure because that's where we keep the tigers.

ROB

We can't put the 20 wolves in with the tigers!

JANE

No, it's OK they'll be gone by Friday, we've sold them to the circus.

ROB

Have we? Whose idea was that?

JANE

Yours. We needed money to buy some new animals…some wolves.

ROB

Wolves are a great idea. What do you think your goal is now?

Bob writes, 'By next Friday, we will be able to keep 20 wolves on the estate, separately and safely from the sheep.' ROB

Perfect!

ROB

It's a bit better than "Putting up a fence." Let's go then.

As I reflected upon the vivid dream I had written down, an intriguing realisation dawned upon me. It held within it the potential to unravel something profound, a puzzle waiting to be solved. However, I didn't immediately delve into deciphering its meaning. Instead, I allowed it to simmer in the depths of my mind, waiting for the right time for its revelation.

After some time had passed, the puzzle pieces began to align, and I saw an opportunity to transform this enigmatic dream into something practical and impactful. The notion of turning it into a workshop on goal setting took hold of my thoughts. It seemed fitting, as the dream had sparked a process of introspection and exploration within me, and perhaps it could do the same for others.

With a sense of curiosity and a touch of trepidation, I decided to test the workshop concept with a small group. It was an experiment, an opportunity to iterate and refine the ideas that had sprouted from that dream. As the workshop unfolded, I witnessed the participants' engagement and their growing enthusiasm for the material.

The workshop became a platform for shared experiences, where individuals from diverse backgrounds and levels of expertise came together to explore the intricacies of collaboration and goal setting. It transcended the boundaries of a simple training session, evolving into a transformative journey for each participant.

What fascinated me the most was the surprising consistency in the conclusions drawn by the participants, regardless of their prior experience. It seemed as though an intuitive understanding emerged within the group, transcending individual perspectives and converging on a shared understanding of the pitfalls of failed collaboration.

The participants began to piece together the story of Rob and Jane, hypothesising that Rob had likely provided instructions to Jane without offering much context or room for clarification. Their collective insight shed light on the importance of clear communication, active questioning, and the need for a shared understanding of goals and expectations.

With each iteration of the workshop, I witnessed its impact on the participants. It sparked introspection, prompting individuals to examine their own communication and collaboration practices. It encouraged them to question assumptions, challenge traditional approaches, and embrace a more open and inclusive mindset.

Over time, word spread about the workshop's effectiveness, and more people sought to participate, including new starters eager to embark on their own journeys within the organisation. It became a rite of passage, a foundational experience that provided a solid footing for individuals as they navigated the complexities of their roles and the dynamics of teamwork.

To this day, I am frequently approached to facilitate this workshop, a testament to its enduring relevance and impact. It has become a cornerstone of my leadership journey, a reminder of the power of introspection, intuition, and the willingness to share our experiences for the benefit of others.

As I guide participants through the workshop, I am reminded of the transformative power of dreams and the untapped potential that lies within our subconscious minds. I am humbled by the opportunity to facilitate meaningful connections, to ignite a spark of self-discovery within each participant, and to witness their growth as they navigate their own collaborative endeavours.

Here is a sample of what groups typically come up with when I ask the groups to work back through the scene and detail the mistakes that both Rob and Jane have made.

Rob's Mistakes

Wasn't clear on the overall vision and didn't share it.

Asking the wrong and irrelevant questions (Especially his opening questions. What does it look like?)

His responses just weren't detailed enough.

Doesn't question what additional work is involved or what the work is.

Distraction and loss of focus on the conversation and what's important.

Forgetful.

Didn't describe the overall goal.

He omitted relevant/important details.

Thought he knew the best way to achieve the goals.

He didn't track what Bob was doing.

Assumed Bob knew what the fence was for.

There was no communication during the task.

I didn't say what the reason for the fence was—no overall big goal.

Didn't give a reason for the date or a clear purpose.

Assumed they needed a fence.

Didn't confirm the plan.

Measures success using a variety of unimportant criteria.

Misses the big picture.

Didn't explain the problem or why they were doing it.

Specified a task rather than a goal (and his task doesn't even solve his problem).

Appears whimsical and without clear direction. What's his long-term plan?

Jumped straight to task without sharing goal, should have identified top-level goal.

Didn't look at the broader picture when defining work, should have shared full context with Bob.

Asked "How does it look?" first, which has nothing to do with the goal really.

Didn't clarify just how wrong Bob was when he built a wooden fence around the field.

Continue to allow tasks to develop without a specification.

Jane's Mistakes

Wasn't asking why or what it was for?

Made a lot of assumptions and acted on them without verifying.

Eager to act without confirming.

Did not ask questions (e.g. when, purpose, specific requirements) made assumptions.

Didn't communicate the plan he made or invite feedback on it.

Waited until job was completed before reviewing with client.

Didn't ask, "Why?" couldn't validate if tasks were appropriate.

Assumed Robot Guy shared his taste in wood.

Too eager. Runs off without any plan, making the same mistakes as before (resource mismanagement).

Did it immediately, used all the wood without review.

No time expectation for delivery: surprised by the Friday deadline.

Too eager to run off and start working.

Doesn't know (hasn't checked) reason for doing the work.

Makes decisions on requirements without checking.

Didn't question why she was doing the task.

Too eager to run off and start working.

Preoccupied with form over function.

Doesn't care about cost, yet they are cost-constrained (as they had to sell the tigers).

Didn't fully understand or make sure what was required before doing work.

Wants to get going too quickly.

Think more resources are necessary without understanding.

Should have made sure goal was agreed before undertaking the work by asking questions.

It's a pretty powerful list for a short exchange that came in a dream! There are so many day-to-day failures of workplace interactions between someone who wants to get something done and the person doing it.

After these have been fed back to the group, we discuss together a number of questions:

What should each have done differently?

What do we think of the initial goals they agreed on?

What other goals are considered? What would have happened if the conversation had ended there?

What do you think the relationship is between Jane and Rob?

Who is more at fault for the wasted work? Can you improve on the goals they agree on?

After this conversation, what is the goal?

What work is actually required?

Should Rob or Jane decide?

What do you think will happen next?

Is person likely to be disappointed?

What should happen to Westfield?

From these discussions we get to a hierarchy of goals: the first that they agreed on before this scene, the remainder that they progressively stumble towards within it.

Instruction	Build a fence
Task	We have barbed wires in the west field that divides the field in half.
Vision-free goals	Keep the wolves away from the sheep in the West Field.
Overly specific/overly vague goal	By next Friday, we will be able to keep 20 wolves on the estate safely and separately from the sheep.
Powerful Goals	By next Friday, we will be able to keep 20 wolves on the estate safely.

Powerful Goals Allow Us to Manage the Outcome Not the Output

Imagine a group of leaders who possess a unique brand of ambition—one that is not self-centred but rather directed towards empowering their team members. These leaders understand that true success lies not in controlling every aspect of their team's work but in nurturing an environment of empowerment and growth.

Instead of obsessing over micromanaging every output, these ambitious leaders focus on managing the outcome—the overarching goals and vision that drive their team forward. They trust their team members' expertise, creativity, and potential, and they provide them with the necessary resources, support, and guidance to thrive. These are powerful goals, as described above, that allow these leaders to achieve them by contracting effectively with team members.

Their ambition is not centred on personal glory or individual achievements. Instead, it is fuelled by a genuine desire to ignite the fire within others—to inspire and motivate their team members to reach new heights of excellence. They understand that true leadership lies in empowering others to shine.

These leaders create a culture that values collaboration, autonomy, and personal development. They foster an atmosphere where team members feel safe to take risks, explore their own ideas, and push beyond their comfort zones. They recognise that by nurturing individual flames within their team, they can collectively ignite a powerful fire of collective success.

As ambitious leaders, they set high standards and expectations, not to exert control, but to challenge and stretch their team members' capabilities. They provide constructive feedback and guidance, helping their team members develop the skills and competencies necessary to excel in their roles. They celebrate achievements and milestones along the way, recognising the hard work and dedication of their team.

These leaders understand that their role is not to be the sole driving force behind success, but rather to be a catalyst—an empowering force that unlocks the untapped potential within each team member. They create opportunities for growth, provide mentorship, and foster an environment where everyone feels valued and empowered to contribute their unique talents and perspectives.

Through their ambitious leadership, they inspire others to believe in themselves and their capabilities. They cultivate a sense of ownership and pride within their team, as each individual realises their integral role in the collective success of the organisation.

In this ambitious leadership paradigm, success is not measured solely by individual achievements but by the growth, fulfilment, and accomplishments of the entire team. These leaders understand that by empowering others, they can create a ripple effect of positive impact that extends far beyond their own ambitions.

So let us aspire to be these ambitious leaders—to shift our focus from control to empowerment, to ignite the fire within others, and to enable them to reach new heights of success. Together, we can create a world where ambitious leadership is synonymous with empowering leadership and where the collective achievements of our teams shine brighter than any individual accolades.

Key Points

- Ambitious leaders focus on empowering their team members rather than controlling every aspect of their work.
- They manage the outcome, not the output, by setting powerful goals that drive their team forward.
- Their ambition is centred on inspiring and motivating others to reach new heights of excellence.
- They create a culture that values collaboration, autonomy, and personal development.
- Ambitious leaders challenge and stretch their team members' capabilities while providing support and guidance.
- They unlock the untapped potential within each team member and foster a sense of ownership and pride.
- Success is measured by the growth, fulfilment, and accomplishments of the entire team, not just individual achievements.
- Ambitious leadership is about empowering others and creating a ripple effect of positive impact.

Pillar #5 Timely Feedback

Key Practice: Tell the microscopic truth.

Oh, would some power the gift gives us.
To see ourselves as others see us.
It would, from many a blunder, free us.
And foolish notion.

Robert Burns: 'To a Louse'.

I enjoy meeting with people I manage or mentor on a monthly basis for about 45 minutes to an hour. During these meetings, I like to reflect on their performance, focusing on what they have accomplished. However, I believe that most of the feedback on their performance should be provided at the moment, so the monthly meetings are mainly for summarising and discussing their behaviour.

I strongly believe that behaviour is what sets someone apart and allows them to go from being good to being great. While competence is important, it is ultimately one's behaviour that makes a significant difference. Emotional intelligence (EI) plays a fundamental role in managing our behaviour. According to Daniel Goleman's influential 2004 Harvard Business Review article, 'What Makes a Leader,' emotional intelligence is twice as important as technical smarts at all job levels, and it accounts for nearly 90% of the difference between average and star performers, particularly in top-tier positions.

Numerous studies have supported Goleman's findings, showing a correlation between higher emotional intelligence and better managerial and leadership performance. One notable example is the research on emotional intelligence and leadership effectiveness conducted by Robert Kerr, John Garvin, Norma Heaton, and Emily Boyle. Developing our own emotional intelligence is crucial, but we also need feedback to refine our social awareness, relationship management skills, and better understand how our behaviour impacts others.

When it comes to providing feedback, I follow Brene Brown's mantra from 'Dare to Lead': "Clear is kind, and unclear is unkind." It is important to be transparent and explicit with the people we manage or mentor, not only about their performance and results but also about their behaviour. However, being clear can sometimes be challenging on a personal level, and it may be tempting to fall into the trap of being 'nice' instead of being clear. To move beyond mere niceties and into true compassion, I remind myself of the universal need for feedback. If feedback is delivered compassionately, with the intention of helping someone become their best self and fostering their growth, then I firmly believe that everyone would want to know the truth about themselves.

Feedback for development and recognition, which helps combat imposter syndrome, serves different purposes, and requires different settings. Public recognition and private feedback are both vital services we can offer to our team members. People deserve to hear the truth, and it should be shared with them compassionately.

In my personal journey, I have worked on improving my relationships, and one book that had a profound impact on me is 'Conscious Loving: The Journey to Co-Commitment' by Gay and Kathlyn Hendricks.

Within the book, I discovered the concept of telling the microscopic truth, which is highly relevant to the relationship between a manager and their team members in the workplace. Telling the microscopic truth means speaking honestly about your internal experience as you perceive it in the moment. By sharing raw data about your thoughts and emotions, you can foster healing and understanding.

The Hendricks explain why people often fail to tell the truth, either by actively lying or passively withholding it. These reasons also apply to the workplace. One reason is the fear of hurting another person's feelings, but in reality, the stronger reason is often the avoidance of dealing with the potential negative emotions that may arise as a consequence. This is a common occurrence in the workplace, where individuals may avoid addressing issues like a colleague's chronic lateness to meetings because they don't want to deal with the person's reaction. Instead, they tolerate the behaviour.

Another reason for avoiding truth-telling is that many people have rarely experienced the truth being spoken to them, nor have they had good examples from which to learn. This lack of exposure to compassionate truth extends to company culture as well. Many individuals have never received compassionate feedback or been trained on how to provide effective feedback.

To help myself be honest with both myself and others, I carry a definition of telling the microscopic truth at work. I share only versions of events that are undeniably true and defensible in a court of law. What is undeniable is my personal experience, and each of us is the leading authority on our own experience.

For example, suppose you are leading someone who frequently expresses strong, closed opinions that hinder group collaboration. Providing feedback that is not the microscopic truth would be saying, "You stop other people in the group from contributing." This feedback can be argued in a court of law, as there could be multiple reasons why people choose not to contribute in a group setting, and it may not solely be the fault of the individual receiving the feedback. Moreover, this feedback lacks compassion and reflects a victim mindset that sees everything as broken.

In contrast, a compassionate telling of the microscopic truth might be, "When you stated so strongly that no one will ever use the feature I suggested, I felt like I didn't want to share any more ideas. It is possible that the other members of the group felt the same way." This type of feedback is likely to initiate a discussion about the individual's feelings and the underlying reasons for expressing such strong, closed opinions. Only after this discussion can a coaching point be made, such as,

"Expressing points of view clearly and respectfully is valuable in our work, but if you could find a way to show some doubt and be open to evidence that might prove us wrong, the group as a whole might become more productive."

In my experience, performance and behaviour are not linearly related but instead exist on a circular spectrum. It is better to view them as interconnected and adjacent to each other. I have found it universally applicable to recognise that an excess of one's greatest strength can become their greatest weakness.

For instance, an excellent technical problem solver may struggle to develop the individuals they lead because they tend to solve all their problems for them. A highly regarded designer who excels at synthesising multiple viewpoints may miss the moment when direction needs to be provided. A reflective thinker may hesitate to take action when the time is right. An instinctive decision-maker may miss out on the benefits of exploring alternative options.

Identifying the tipping point where our strengths begin to hinder our intentions is challenging to do alone. This is where compassionate truth becomes incredibly valuable. It allows us to gain insight and self-awareness, enabling personal growth and improvement.

Key points

- Behaviour is what sets someone apart and allows them to go from being good to being great.
- Emotional intelligence (EI) is twice as important as technical smarts and plays a significant role in managing behaviour.
- Feedback is crucial for refining social awareness, relationship management skills, and understanding the impact of our behaviour on others.
- Feedback should be clear and explicit, transparently addressing performance and behaviour.
- It is important to provide feedback compassionately with the intention of fostering growth and helping individuals become their best selves.
- Feedback about development and recognition serve different purposes and should be delivered in different settings.
- 'Telling the microscopic truth' involves speaking honestly about internal experiences to foster healing and understanding.
- People often avoid telling the truth due to fear of hurting feelings or dealing with potential negative emotions.
- Many people lack exposure to compassionate truth and haven't received effective feedback.
- Telling the microscopic truth involves sharing undeniably true and defensible personal experiences.
- Performance and behaviour are interconnected and exist on a circular spectrum.
- Excess of one's greatest strength can become their greatest weakness.
- Compassionate truth enables insight, self-awareness, personal growth, and improvement.

Pillar #6 A-ha Discovery

Key Practice: Create psychological safety.

Greet what you learn with an 'ah ha' not an 'oh no'.
**Gay and Kathlyn Hendricks, Conscious Loving:
The Journey to Co-Commitment.**

Psychological Safety As a Service to Your Team

Amy Edmondson stumbled into the discovery that led her to first coin the term 'Psychological Safety' when she was part of an interdisciplinary group studying medication errors in hospitals in the mid-1990s. In her excellent book, "The Fearless Organisation: Creating Psychological Safety in the Workplace for Learning, Innovation, and Growth," she both lays out what it is and how we as leaders can foster it.

What Is Psychological Safety?

As Edmonson says, "Psychological safety describes a climate where people feel safe enough to take interpersonal risks by speaking up and sharing concerns, questions, or ideas." It does not mean everyone is "nice." You will get more feedback in a psychologically safe environment than in a less safe one, but you will be more comfortable receiving it and providing it because you will know it is not feedback on you but instead on the work you have contributed to.

Importantly, psychological safety is also not about relaxing performance standards but rather about creating a learning environment.

	LOW demand	HIGH demand
HIGH Psychological Safety	Comfort Zone	**Learning Zone**
LOW Psychological Safety	Apathy Zone	Anxiety Zone

Source: Amy Edmondsen.

Leaders' role in building psychological safety

The Fearless Organisation gives us three key actions for building **psychological safety:**

1. Set the stage and frame the work.
2. Invite engagement.
3. Respond appreciatively.

Of course, the whole team needs to care about the product they are making or the service they are delivering, but the whole team needs to be united around a single purpose. It is this framing that gives people a shared understanding of the work they will do to create it. In the game they are making, we need to build a coherent experience for our players that serves both a creative and a business purpose, not ship them a box of collected ideas. It's not enough for each individual to do what he or she cares about the most, and it becomes problematic when individuals are pursuing excellence in their craft as a higher priority than what is right for the game. In a game, this would manifest as artists modelling details that players will never ever see, designers creating game mechanics that suit only their personal play style, and programmers writing new code where existing functionality could be reused.

As leaders, we need to draw upon all our personal development in personal authenticity, quiet ego, and patience with yourself and others to identify and help the team identify for themselves all the instincts that will have to be noticed, accepted, and chosen not to identify with if we are to be successful. Equally all those skills will be needed to create a case for speaking up and the consistency of treating people compassionately that encourages engagement and speaking up that is needed and to respond appreciatively to them when they do.

The Only Real Failure Is Failure to Learn

As a game team, we looked to constantly reevaluate the scope and priority of what we understood is needed to complete the next release of the game. We needed to get round the 'Build->Play->Review->Change->Repeat' as often and as quickly as possible. So as leaders or facilitators of the review, our attitude was important to set an attitude of learning.

Fearless Organisation again gave us a powerful distinction between types of failure:

- Preventable "where we know how to do it right."
- Complex "where complex factors combine in novel ways to produce failures in reasonably familiar contexts."
- Intelligent "the undesired results of forays into novel territory."

Our leaders needed to draw a distinction between the types of errors and respond to them accordingly, which was critical to building psychological safety. Here's the best practice:

- Reduce preventable failures.
- Anticipate and mitigate complex failures.
- Celebrate intelligent failures.

We needed to recognise preventable and complex failures to get the major value that could come from intelligent failures.

The Benefits of 'Ah Ha' over 'Oh No' in Celebrating Intelligent Failures

When we are reviewing and we don't get what we expect, how do we react? I believe if we can acknowledge our impulse to judge but not identify with it for a little while, there is an opportunity to mine much gold. In complex game projects, many of the best features are discovered by accident. Post-its were discovered when 3M was looking for the strongest adhesive possible. Scientist August Kekule uncovered the ring structure of benzene when he dreamt of a snake biting its own tail. So many features that make games great can be discovered when looking for something else...a 'bug' that creates x-ray mode, for instance.

During my personal development, I came across the parable of the Chinese farmer. There are many versions of the story, but here is the version I remember:

Once, there was a Chinese farmer. He tended his meagre farm with his son and their single horse. One day, the horse ran off. People from their village came by and said to the farmer, "How unfortunate for you!" The farmer replied, "Maybe so, maybe not."

The horse returned a few days later and was followed by a whole herd of wild horses. The villagers said to the farmer, "What good luck for you!" The farmer replied, "Maybe so, maybe not."

The son started work, trying to tame the wild horses, but he fell and broke his leg. He couldn't work on the farm. "How unlucky for you," the villagers said to the farmer, "Maybe so, maybe not," he said.

The next week, the army came to recruit young men for a campaign in which many young men had already died. They let the farmer's son be when they saw his broken leg. The villagers said to the farmer, "What good luck for your son!" "Maybe so, maybe not," was all the farmer said.

I have 'maybe so, maybe not' stencilled onto a stair riser in my house to remind me to meet life's events in a spirit of learning without identifying with my instinctive judgement. This is what I found I needed to bring to review to create a celebration and squeeze the learning from intelligent failures.

Key Points

- Psychological safety is a climate where people feel safe to take interpersonal risks and share concerns, questions, or ideas. Psychological safety is not about being "nice," but about creating a learning environment.
- Leaders play a crucial role in building psychological safety by setting the stage, inviting engagement, and responding appreciatively.

- The framing of a shared purpose is essential to unite the team and create a coherent experience.
- Personal authenticity, quiet ego, and patience are necessary for leaders to identify instincts, encourage engagement, and respond compassionately.
- Failure should be categorised as preventable, complex, or intelligent, and each type should be addressed accordingly.
- Preventable failures should be reduced, complex failures should be anticipated and mitigated, and intelligent failures should be celebrated.
- Celebrating intelligent failures can lead to unexpected discoveries and innovations.
- The parable of the Chinese farmer teaches the importance of approaching life's events with a spirit of learning and without immediate judgement.

Pillar #7 Personal Authenticity

Key Practice: Meaningful connection.

Be yourself; everyone else is taken.

Oscar Wilde.

Armed with my newfound understanding of "I am awareness," I realised that personal authenticity would be the core of my journey towards a healthier and more sustainable leadership style that truly serves the people I lead. I couldn't bear to wear a mask any longer.

But what does personal authenticity mean? Luther Price's quote beautifully encapsulates the case against pretending and hypocrisy: "Be what you is, not what you ain't; 'cause if you ain't what you is you ais what you ain't."

Naturally, the path to personal authenticity often involves staying true to ourselves, being who we truly are, and not pretending to be someone else. However, as Hermina Ibarra points out in her insightful TEDx Talk on The Authenticity Paradox, this raises an important question: which version of ourselves should we be true to? Our past self, our current self, or our future ideal self?

For me, personal authenticity means committing to act in alignment with my true values at all times. It doesn't mean I have to express every thought without a filter, nor does it prevent me from performing in order to coach or inspire others. It means always sharing my truth as I experience it, infused with compassion. It means that when I perform, I am selecting the aspects of myself that are most appropriate and compassionate for that particular audience.

Personal authenticity also entails a commitment to self-discovery and continuous learning about who I am. As a result, the self I am being true to is constantly evolving.

Moreover, personal integrity is non-negotiable. It means doing the right thing, even when nobody is watching, and nobody will ever find out.

Authenticity is not only an act of compassion towards those we lead but also towards ourselves. In our society, people are searching for purpose and meaning, and they often look for it in the workplace when traditional institutions like churches and communities no longer provide it. Purpose and meaning arise from truth. To provide the truth, we must first be personally authentic. In this context, personal authenticity becomes essential for effective leadership.

Choosing to model authenticity is a truly compassionate act. It establishes the principle that in the workplace, it is acceptable to be your genuine self and that everyone is free to bring their whole selves to work. This was, and continues to be, a crucial aspect for me: creating an environment where everyone, including myself, can bring their authentic selves. I firmly believe that this is vital for cultivating a high-performing team.

Being true to yourself, in addition to showing compassion towards those you lead, is the ultimate act of self-compassion. Pretending to be someone you are not is exhausting and drains your energy. Embracing authenticity demonstrates to those we lead that growth comes from being genuine and not from pretence.

The commitment to self-discovery, which is essential for personal authenticity, is far from comfortable. It is much easier to stick with familiar behaviours that provide a sense of security, even if they no longer serve us. Reaching out to connect with others as our true selves can be scary, as it involves the risk of rejection, whether real or perceived. However, as Brene Brown's work teaches us, "Vulnerability is the birthplace of creativity, innovation, and change." If we want to grow, we must embrace the advice of humanistic psychologist Abraham Maslow: choose growth over safety and overcome fear repeatedly.

Yet, there is another fear that sometimes acts as a barrier to authenticity, and we may resist acknowledging it. Embracing authenticity and accepting our true selves may require forgiving ourselves, which can be more challenging than it initially sounds. It involves engaging in a candid conversation with ourselves, taking an honest look at our past behaviours, and acknowledging the pain we may have caused others and ourselves.

However, in my experience, it is worth the effort. Others' forgiveness cannot truly touch us until we are ready to forgive ourselves.

Engaging in this self-forgiveness work sets us up for a healthier and happier state of being. As Dr Tim Cantopher reminds us in *Overcoming Stress: Advice for People Who Give Too Much*, "the smaller the distance between our ideal self and our real self, the healthier and happier we will be."

Authentic leaders inspire and connect on a deep level.

Authentic leaders have a remarkable ability to inspire and forge meaningful connections with those around them. They possess a genuine presence that emanates from their true selves, drawing others in and fostering a sense of trust and admiration. When leaders are authentic, people are naturally inspired to follow their lead, as they can sense the authenticity in their words and actions.

Embrace your uniqueness, for it is your true self that resonates with others.

Each person possesses a unique combination of experiences, values, strengths, and quirks that make them who they are. Embracing and celebrating one's uniqueness is a powerful act of self-acceptance. When individuals embrace their true selves and bring their authentic selves to the table, they radiate a genuine aura that resonates with others. It is this authenticity that creates a deep and lasting connection with those they interact with.

Let's create a culture of authenticity where vulnerability is celebrated and individuality flourishes.

In our pursuit of fostering a culture of authenticity, we must create an environment where vulnerability is not only accepted but celebrated. When individuals feel safe to be vulnerable and open about their thoughts, feelings, and experiences, it cultivates an atmosphere of trust and openness. This allows for genuine connections to form and for individuality to flourish, as people are encouraged to bring their true selves to the forefront without fear of judgement or rejection.

By promoting and nurturing authenticity, we create a space where each person can shine in their own unique way, contributing their strengths and perspectives to the collective whole. In such a culture, individuals are empowered to express themselves authentically, leading to increased creativity, innovation, and collaboration.

People Are Yearning for Purpose and Meaning in Their Lives.

In the midst of the chaos and demands of modern life, many individuals find themselves searching for something more profound—a deep sense of purpose and meaning. They yearn for a greater sense of fulfilment and a connection to something that transcends the daily grind. It's as if their souls are crying out for a purpose that brings them joy and gives their lives a profound sense of significance.

When we live in alignment with our truth—our authentic selves—we unlock the potential for purpose and meaning to blossom in our lives. It is when we honour our core values, passions, and aspirations that we tap into a source of deep fulfilment and a profound sense of purpose. Living authentically allows us to navigate life with integrity, aligning our actions and choices with our innermost beliefs and values.

To provide others with truth, we must first be personally authentic. Personal authenticity is about being true to ourselves, embracing our unique qualities, and expressing our genuine thoughts and feelings. It requires the courage to show up as our true selves, without pretence or masks. When we are personally authentic, we create an environment of trust and openness, enabling us to share the truth with others in a genuine and meaningful way.

By embodying personal authenticity, we become conduits of truth for those around us. Our words and actions carry the weight of authenticity, resonating with others on a deep level. When we are true to ourselves, we are better equipped to provide guidance, support, and wisdom based on our own lived experiences and genuine perspectives.

Ultimately, personal authenticity is the bridge that connects us to truth, allowing us to offer others the guidance and insights they seek. It is through our own journey of self-discovery and living authentically that we become beacons of truth, illuminating the path to purpose, and meaning for ourselves and those we encounter along the way.

Key Points

- Personal authenticity is at the core of a healthier and more sustainable leadership style.

- Personal authenticity means being true to ourselves and not pretending to be someone else.
- Personal authenticity involves acting in alignment with our true values and constantly evolving.
- Personal integrity is essential to maintaining authenticity.
- Authenticity is an act of compassion towards others and ourselves.
- Authenticity creates an environment where everyone can bring their authentic selves.
- Being true to oneself is an act of self-compassion and promotes growth.
- Embracing authenticity requires self-forgiveness and acceptance.
- Authentic leaders inspire and connect on a deep level.
- Embracing uniqueness and celebrating individuality is important.
- Creating a culture of authenticity involves celebrating vulnerability and nurturing individuality.
- Authenticity contributes to purpose and meaning in life.
- Living authentically allows for integrity and aligning actions with values.
- Personal authenticity enables us to provide truth and guidance to others.
- Personal authenticity is the bridge to truth and the path to purpose and meaning.

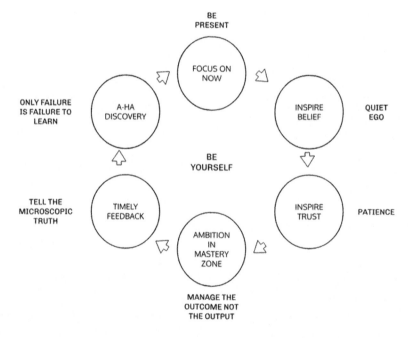

Part 3
Liberated Leadership in Practice

Scaling Up: Creating a Values-Driven Company

Back in the Driving Seat

Towards the end of 2019, the responsibility for developing games for the Need for Speed brand returned to Criterion. It was an exciting time for us as we embarked on a new chapter. In early 2020, we brought together all the incredibly talented individuals based in the UK—from Criterion, Ghost, and EA central groups—to form a larger, unified version of Criterion. The goal was to build upon our past successes and create something even greater. Personally, I saw this as an opportunity to demonstrate liberated leadership in action throughout a two-year development cycle.

However, little did I know that our plans would be drastically impacted by the rapid spread of COVID-19. By March, the virus had become rampant across the UK and the rest of the world, forcing us to adapt to a new reality. Suddenly, we found ourselves working from home, facing a unique set of challenges that tested not only our approach and values as a team but also our individual resilience.

The global pandemic presented us with unforeseen obstacles, but it also became a catalyst for growth and adaptation. We had to find innovative ways to collaborate remotely, maintain our sense of camaraderie, and ensure the well-being of each team member. It became a journey of discovering how to navigate through uncertainty while staying true to our vision and values.

Amidst the chaos and uncertainty, we learned the true strength of our team and the power of our collective spirit. We supported one another, finding solace and motivation in our shared purpose. The experience highlighted the importance of flexibility, resilience, and empathy as we adjusted to the new work-from-home reality.

While the pandemic presented unforeseen challenges, it also gave us an opportunity to reevaluate our approach and develop new strategies for success. We embraced the need for adaptability and pushed ourselves to find creative solutions to the unique problems we faced. The experience served as a reminder of the strength and determination that exist within each of us when faced with adversity.

As we moved forward, I remained committed to the vision of liberated leadership and strived to create an environment where everyone felt empowered, even in the face of unprecedented circumstances. I recognised that true leadership is not about control but about fostering a sense of trust, autonomy, and collaboration.

Through it all, we grew as individuals and as a team. We discovered new depths of resilience, adaptability, and compassion. The journey was challenging, but it reinforced the belief that when we come together, support one another, and stay true to our values, we can overcome any obstacle that comes our way.

As we continued through our development cycle, we carried out the lessons learned during this period with us. The experience had shaped us, reminding us of the importance of staying agile, embracing change, and nurturing a culture of collaboration and authenticity. Together, we were prepared to face whatever challenges lay ahead, united by our shared purpose and unwavering determination to create something truly extraordinary.

New studio, common values.

As we embarked on our journey with the new studio, we recognised the importance of establishing common values that would guide us in our work and interactions. As we synthesised from the three uniting groups, our values became clear to us:

- **We value iterative improvement in how we work and play together.**
- **We value growth as people and as game makers.**
- **We value living, playing, and working with passion and commitment.**
- **We value the power of the team over individual heroism.**

Translating these values into tangible behaviours, we identified our 'superpowers' that would bring our values to life:

1. **Because we value living, playing, and working with passion and commitment, we love games, and we love making games.** Our enthusiasm for games is infectious, fuelling our dedication and driving us to create exceptional experiences.

2. **Because we value the power of the team over individual heroism, we favour creative, energetic collaboration.** We thrive in an environment that encourages diverse perspectives and harnesses the collective power of our team's talents.

3. **Because we value growth as people and as game makers, we're generous, responsibly open, and transparent.** We embrace continuous learning and growth, sharing our knowledge and experiences to elevate ourselves and others.

4. **We value iterative improvement in how we work and play together, and we love to find what's good about an idea and bring positive energy to make it even better.** We foster an atmosphere of constructive feedback and celebrate incremental progress, always seeking ways to refine and enhance our work.

In addition, we encouraged curiosity to challenge conventions in people, products, and processes. We approached unfamiliar or disliked aspects with a presumption of positive intent, seeking understanding, and finding common ground.

These values and behaviours served as the foundation for our studio culture. They guided us in our daily interactions, ensuring that we approached our work with passion, collaboration, growth, and a relentless commitment to improvement. By embracing these values and superpowers, we were poised to create remarkable games and cultivate an environment where every individual could thrive and contribute their best. The world, however, had other plans.

COVID Crisis: Business Unusual

On Friday, March 13th, 2020, a day forever etched in my memory, I woke up to a message from EA Leadership in San Francisco. It was a message that would change the course of our work and lives. The message stated that none of us were to attend the office until further notice. Little did we know that this was just the beginning of a challenging and unprecedented journey.

Just one week later, the entire UK went into a national lockdown. Our world shifted drastically, and we found ourselves facing the daunting task of reinventing our working practices to adapt to remote work. It was a moment of realisation that this was no ordinary time—it was business unusual.

In those early days of remote work, we did our best to recreate our office routines through platforms like Zoom. But it quickly became apparent that we needed to go beyond simply replicating our previous ways of working. We needed to find new approaches and strategies to navigate this unfamiliar territory.

One meeting that immediately took on heightened significance was our 'Start the Week' session every Monday at 10 am. It became the anchor for our studio, providing a vital touchpoint for connection and communication. During these sessions, I would share updates on the company's response to the COVID-19 pandemic, offering guidance and support to our team. Another member of our studio leadership would bring everyone up to speed on the progress of our project, grounding us in the work that still needed to be done.

Early on at Start the Week, we shared four principles from EA Leadership that would define our approach:

#1 Our mental, emotional, and physical health and supporting our families are a higher priority than optimising productivity or anything else right now.

#2 We are part of an organisation that cares about us.

#3 Our team will not be judged in the same way as it would be when things were normal.

#4 Now more than ever, we need each other's support.

These virtual gatherings became more than just routine check-ins. They became moments of connection and reassurance. We shared our concerns, celebrated small victories, and provided much-needed encouragement to one another. It was during these meetings that we realised the importance of empathy and compassion in supporting each other through this challenging time.

As we navigated the uncharted waters of remote work, we faced numerous obstacles and uncertainties. But through it all, our commitment to the well-being and growth of our team remained steadfast. We adapted to new technologies, found innovative ways to collaborate from a distance, and continually learned from our experiences.

While the pandemic forced us apart physically, it also brought us closer in many ways. We learned to lean on one another and to offer support and understanding when someone was facing challenges. We became a virtual community, united in our shared purpose and determination to overcome the obstacles before us.

Looking back, I am grateful for the resilience and adaptability that emerged from our team during this time. We learned that true leadership is not about controlling every detail but about fostering a sense of connection and providing the support needed to navigate through uncertainty. It was a reminder that even in the most trying circumstances, we have the power to come together, support one another, and find new ways to thrive.

Asynchronous Communication

When the shift to remote work occurred, one of the immediate changes we noticed was the surge in asynchronous communication. Discussions that were once held face-to-face now took place in lengthy Slack threads or through comments on Google Slides and Docs. However, this change brought forth a new challenge—we realised that these written comments lacked the tone of voice we were accustomed to. Without nonverbal cues, intentions could easily be misinterpreted, leading to potential misunderstandings.

To address this, we recognised the importance of expressing ourselves with utmost clarity, compassion, self-responsibility, and a focus on the common good. We established four key principles to guide healthy asynchronous communication:

- **Keep it impersonal; it's about what, not who.** By focusing on the issue at hand rather than personalising it, we create a space for constructive dialogue and problem-solving.
- **State your assumptions to provide context for your comments.** Sharing the assumptions underlying our thoughts helps others understand the reasoning behind our suggestions or concerns. For example, we may preface our comment with "assuming that this thing is true, we may need to make this change."
- **Avoid being accidentally declaratively certain.** Instead of making absolute statements, we strive to express uncertainty or seek clarification. This encourages open-mindedness and invites

collaboration. For instance, saying, "Is this achievable with current constraints?" or "AFAIK, this cannot be done within current constraints," fosters a more productive conversation than a definitive "this is impossible."

- **Check for intention and seek clarity.** Whenever we encounter a comment or message that may be open to interpretation, we take the time to seek clarification.

Questions like "Does this mean...?", "Are you assuming...?", or "What is the context here?" Help us understand the intended meaning and avoid misunderstandings.

In addition to these principles, we encouraged intentional overcommunication. Asynchronous communication tends to be slower than face-to-face interactions, so we recognised the need to provide more detailed information than we were accustomed to. We established six principles to guide our approach:

- **Don't worry about stating the obvious.** It's better to include information that may seem redundant than to assume it's already known by everyone.
- **Supplement your explanation with images and screenshots.** Visual aids can enhance understanding and provide clarity.
- **Annotate images and screenshots to highlight relevant portions**. By drawing attention to specific areas, we ensure that our message aligns with what we want to convey.
- **Always provide precise details about dates and times.** Mentioning the exact days of the week, times, and time zones helps eliminate ambiguity and ensures everyone is on the same page.
- **Link to references and related discussions whenever possible.** By providing links to relevant information, we make it easier for others to access the context and follow the conversation thread.
- **Organise information for easy consumption.** Structuring our messages and documents in a logical and coherent manner enables others to navigate the content more effectively.

By adhering to these principles, we strive to create an environment of effective and considerate asynchronous communication. We recognise the importance of clear and detailed messaging, as it fosters understanding, collaboration, and a sense of unity even when we are physically apart. Together, we can navigate the challenges of remote work and ensure that our communication remains open, inclusive, and productive.

Managing Cognitive Load

During this time, I stumbled upon the fascinating work of Bluma Wulfovna Zeigarnik, a Russian psychologist who conducted an intriguing experiment in the 1920s. Her findings shed light on how our minds remember incomplete tasks more vividly than those that have been successfully completed. This phenomenon, now known as the Zeigarnik effect, intrigued me as I contemplated its relevance in our new world of asynchronous communication.

In our digitally interconnected environment, it became all too easy to have multiple threads of communication open simultaneously. These ongoing discussions and unfinished tasks could linger in our minds, overwhelming us with an ever-growing mental load. We found ourselves constantly juggling unfinished business, striving to keep track of a multitude of open threads.

While some interruptions were beyond our control, I realised that we also had the power to interrupt ourselves by initiating numerous threads of thought. These self-interruptions could further burden our already overloaded minds. It became clear that we needed a mindful approach to counteract this effect and regain a sense of focus and clarity.

This realisation prompted us to embrace the practice of 'Being present' in the focus phase of liberated leadership. We made a deliberate intention to bring our attention to the present moment, seizing opportunities to finish threads of thought and close them mentally. By consciously completing tasks or finding natural breakpoints, we could release ourselves from the weight of unfinished business.

The practice of being present allowed us to cultivate a deeper sense of mindfulness and awareness in our work. It helped us recognise the importance of fully engaging with the task at hand rather than being scattered across multiple threads. We learned to prioritise and manage our time and attention more effectively, reducing mental clutter and enhancing our ability to focus.

As we became more intentional about finishing threads and bringing closure to our thoughts, we experienced a newfound sense of mental clarity and relief.

The practice of being present in the focus phase empowered us to bring our full attention to each task, enabling us to work more efficiently and effectively.

By consciously embracing the present moment, we discovered the power of letting go of unfinished threads and finding completion. This intentional approach not only enhanced our productivity but also nurtured a sense of calm and balance in our asynchronous work environment. We learned the importance of finding closure and setting boundaries for ourselves, allowing us to navigate our tasks with greater ease and peace of mind.

In a world filled with constant distractions and open threads, the practice of being present served as an anchor, helping us to stay focused and grounded. It reminded us to cherish the present moment, to bring closure to unfinished tasks, and to find balance amidst the ever-evolving landscape of asynchronous communication.

More Tasks, Fewer Goals

The journey of aligning and collaborating within our merged studios and adapting to new leadership structures was already going to be a challenge, even without the impact of COVID-19. As we scaled up our operations and expanded our team to AAA size, we were faced with the task of fostering alignment and collaboration on a larger scale. However, the sudden shift to remote work brought about by the pandemic introduced a whole new dimension to this challenge—one that was amplified by the feelings of loneliness and isolation that accompanied working from home.

Loneliness, as Dr Vivek Murthy, author of 'Together' describes it,

is a subjective feeling that we are lacking social connections in our lives. That's the difference between the connections you need and what you feel you have now. What we feel we need might be different for each of us, and so by definition, loneliness is a subjective term. It's in contrast with isolation, which is an objective term.

Even prior to COVID-19, loneliness was already a societal challenge. However, the pandemic exacerbated this issue by further isolating individuals from their workplace communities. With multiple lockdowns imposed in the UK, the sense of disconnection and loneliness became even more pronounced.

Interestingly, we found that our people, in line with broader research, appeared to be more productive when working from home in terms of completing tasks. Perhaps the autonomy over their environment and the elimination of commuting contributed to this increase in task completion. However, we also realised that more tasks completed did not necessarily equate to the achievement of meaningful goals. In fact, we discovered that we were accomplishing more work but achieving fewer significant goals. We were busier, but the true impact and benefit of our efforts were diminishing.

This realisation compelled us to reflect on the balance between productivity and purpose. We recognised the need to prioritise and refocus our efforts on pursuing powerful goals rather than getting caught up in the never-ending cycle of task completion. We understood that mere busyness does not necessarily translate to meaningful achievements or personal fulfilment.

In the face of increased isolation and remote work, we acknowledged the significance of human connection and its role in fostering collaboration and shared purpose. While we strived to maintain safety during these challenging times, we recognised the importance of nurturing social connections and finding innovative ways to stay connected with our colleagues. We actively sought opportunities for virtual collaboration, creating spaces for meaningful interactions that helped combat the sense of loneliness and foster a sense of belonging within our remote work environment.

I believe our people, in line with wider research, were more productive working from home in the sense of completing more tasks. Possibly due to having more autonomy over their environment, possibly by working more instead of commuting. However, more tasks do not necessarily mean more achievement of powerful goals. We found we were completing more tasks but fewer goals. Simply put, we were doing more work for less benefit.

Why?

Anxiety Kills Trust

Passionate individuals, regardless of their actual progress, often felt like they were falling behind. This phenomenon, combined with the prevalence of imposter syndrome among high performers, was further amplified by the anxiety caused by the societal situation. This heightened anxiety not only affected the game development process but also eroded trust and posed a risk of dangerous levels of stress. As we continued to work from home for an extended period of time, the loss of face-to-face connection with our team presented us with multiple challenges. Our ability to align on plans, track effectiveness, and make necessary adjustments was significantly hindered.

Despite observing positive actions and good decision-making in the game development process, our data was not in a state that allowed for effective analysis and trend identification. Some aspects of the game, such as building out the open world, followed a capacity-driven approach, while others, like game modes, required a priority-driven (Agile) approach. The capacity-driven approach involved determining how many features we could ship by dividing the estimated size of the features by the available effort. On the other hand, the priority-driven approach involved sizing features relative to each other and continuously evaluating progress (velocity) to determine how far we would progress through the priority list by the ship date.

Remote work challenges our progress measurement and estimation accuracy. Pandemic-related focus loss disrupted partnerships and communication, hindering progress tracking. Leaders struggled to obtain the necessary information, fuelling anxiety and promoting independent data gathering.

The urge to resort to command and control in times of threat is similar to the instinct to indulge in a sugary snack when we're hungry. It may provide temporary relief and feel right at the moment, but there are long-term consequences. As a leader, I encouraged people to let go of control and embrace inspiration and coaching to liberate themselves and those they lead. However, this was a significant challenge in a world where we received distressing news of colleagues in the hospital and faced a third national lockdown. Leaders themselves struggled to find liberation and guide their teams in such uncertain and challenging circumstances.

From Values to Manifesto

As a studio leadership team, we recognised the importance of the common values we had established but felt the need for something more concrete. We wanted to express how these values translated into our work principles, inspiring our talent. Thus, the idea of the Criterion Manifesto was born. We aimed to unite our team around these principles, allowing individuals to align themselves with this guiding document. While recovering from COVID, it occurred to me to transform the principles into verse. And this is how it emerged…

We are Criterion…
We believe in inspiration, education, coaching,
Facilitation.
There's no place here for intimidation.

People are talent, not resources; they deserve to be.
treated that way.
Process exists to serve people; that's how we make play.
We believe in the balance between invention,
innovation and preservation,

Maximising the outcome for our players is always our intention.
Our plan is always the best wrong we have today.

But planning together is how we find the right way.
Powerful goals, allied with direction and boundaries,
maximise our autonomy and free us from quandaries.

We believe in learning about our game as we make it.
Together with our partners, we regularly reshape it.

Crunch does not work; it hurts our game and our people.
Things we can't get to, we may well put in a sequel.

We believe a good enough decision, made when it's needed, beats a perfect
decision, made when every last point is heeded.

We believe the difference between feedback and direction is vital.
We ask which one we're hearing, regardless of title.

We share our point of view often and early.
To have a discussion that aligns with us most surely.

We play what we've made together to make our game better.
Shared questions and insights help relieve the pressure.

If we are lost, we go back to our values.
When we are true to them, there's no way we can lose.

We are Criterion.
Passion runs through our veins.
We are stronger together. We love to make games.

It felt powerful at the time, and it still does today. We created a video and a microsite to share with the team in January 2022 for people to sign up. It was also a great introduction to who we are for new starters. It felt good to reaffirm who we were and how we wanted to work, but now we had a game to ship.

Unbound

The final year for NFS Unbound approached, bringing with it the challenges of transitioning from in-office to remote to hybrid working. It was clear that our processes needed to be reevaluated in the future. I recognised the importance of fully embracing the Liberated Leadership cycle to deliver a game that would make us proud and meet the business's objectives. Each day, I instinctively and purposefully worked through the cycle, ensuring our commitment to success.

Focusing on It Now. What Do We Need to Do Right Now?

We maintained our focus on improving the player experience by regularly playing the game together and discussing areas for improvement. This constant emphasis on the present moment allowed us to clearly identify what needed to be excluded from the launch version to ensure the quality of the included features. Features that did not receive attention or focus were deemed out of scope. Our producers faced the challenging task of removing these features from the launch, as passionate teams often desire to include everything. Despite the initial difficulty, it was a necessary decision made by the leaders to narrow the scope of the game, ultimately serving the best interests of the team.

Inspiring Belief. Quiet Ego and Listening With Our Hearts

Inspiring belief and fostering a compassionate environment were key priorities for us as a leadership team. We actively sought out diverse perspectives by creating various channels for open communication. Regular surveys allowed for anonymous feedback, while craft group meetings provided opportunities for specific teams, like engineers, to share their insights and challenges. I personally led the "Loop Group," which aimed to establish clear communication between leaders and the creative teams involved in making the game. By triangulating all opinions, we gained valuable context for our game-development process. We also recognised the presence of imposter syndrome among team members, particularly those working on their first game or in new roles. Leaders played a crucial role in providing context and normalising these feelings, while also offering one-on-one support and encouragement. Reminding individuals of their past successes was important in boosting their confidence and belief in their abilities.

Inspiring Trust. Patience With Ourselves and Others

Inspiring trust was a vital aspect of our team dynamics. Our surveys consistently showed high levels of trust and psychological safety within our team, which was a positive foundation to build upon. However, we faced the challenge of managing our own impatience in relation to the player experience. We had a strong desire for the game to be exceptional, but we had to remind ourselves that achieving that level of quality takes time. It was not always a smooth journey, as improvements sometimes resulted in temporary setbacks. This uncertainty could create anxiety, but we relied on our deep reserves of patience and trust in both ourselves and our teams to ultimately deliver the outcome we all desired.

Ambition in Mastery Zone. Managing the Outcome Not the Output

By re-evaluating our approach and placing a renewed emphasis on goal-oriented work, we aimed to restore the balance between productivity and purpose. We encouraged our team members to reflect on their individual goals and align their tasks, accordingly, ensuring that every action contributed to the achievement of meaningful outcomes. This shift allowed us to direct our collective efforts towards making a real impact and deriving greater satisfaction from our work.

Ultimately, our focus shifted from the quantity of tasks completed to the quality of goals achieved. We understood that true accomplishment lies in pursuing powerful objectives, and we prioritised the alignment of our work with those goals. By doing so, we aimed to break free from the cycle of busyness and reclaim the sense of fulfilment that comes from making meaningful progress towards shared objectives.

As the game approached its final stages, our focus intensified. It became crucial to have a precise understanding of the remaining tasks and exercise tighter control over the work being done. In the critical days leading up to the game's release, a single person, often the technical director, would make decisions about which changes should be included. What sets this approach apart from the traditional model is our unwavering commitment to making decisions that prioritise the player's benefit and the overall team's success. Clear and consistent communication in this context was essential throughout the process.

Timely Feedback. Telling the Microscopic Truth

In our new hybrid working environment, one of the most significant rituals we established was the Friday software share. It was a crucial moment at the end of each week, conducted over Zoom. Our creative director would play through our game, selecting different areas based on the team's current focus. As the game was played, the leader would provide commentary, and there would be an ongoing discussion in the Zoom chat. This ritual served multiple purposes: it allowed us to recognise and appreciate the excellent work that had been accomplished during the week while also collectively acknowledging and taking responsibility for areas that still needed improvement. It fostered a sense of shared ownership and progress.

A-ha Discovery. Creating Psychological Safety

As we approached the final stages of development, the process of finalling was all about maximising the speed of discovery. We kept finding what was wrong and prioritising our efforts to fix it. We constantly played through our experience and tried to maximise the time we had left to improve things for the player. Doing this with a spirit of 'a ha' and not 'oh no' took deliberate effort but reaped huge rewards in terms of energy, learning, and velocity as we managed ourselves towards the finish line.

Throughout All of This, Remain Authentic

Above all, amidst the heightened pressure of the final stages, it was crucial to stay connected on a human level and engage in meaningful conversations. We resisted resorting to transactional exchanges and instead sought to truly see and appreciate the whole person in front of us. This approach fuelled my energy and sustained my enthusiasm to complete a game that we could all genuinely take pride in.

Outcome

Throughout the finalling process, we consistently made decisions to focus on game quality and stability at launch, and the team responded impressively. On the review aggregation website Metacritic, the game received the highest rating of a Need for Speed title since 2013 and delivered on all the player sentiment targets at launch that we had agreed with the company. Unbound was a finalist for 'Best Racing Game of the Year' at the DICE Awards and was nominated for 'Outstanding Video Game' at the GLAAD Media Awards for inclusive representation of the LGBTQ community. The review site Eurogamer called the game "The best Need for Speed in a generation!" and Game Informer described it as "One of the most stylish racing games I've played!"

The game was truly unbound, and through all of this the studio picked up another Best Place to Work award from Gamesindustry.biz in 2022.

For me personally, it was immensely satisfying and time to take Liberated Leadership out into the wider world.

Epilogue

Has depression been a curse or a blessing?

For me, this approach to leadership is not a fixed concept but rather a living and evolving philosophy that I continuously apply. It has been shaped by my personal experience with depression, which, although a challenging journey, has provided me with invaluable insights through mindful practice. While I wouldn't wish depression on anyone, I acknowledge the profound lessons it has taught me.

There have been direct benefits that apply to both my personal and professional lives, as described earlier, as well as more indirect ones. For instance, the open-mindedness cultivated in mindful meditation translates to the skill of associative thinking, which is essential for fostering creativity. I have also acquired practices along the way that have enhanced my relationships, both in and outside of work.

When it comes to those I lead, it's important to be honest and admit that I don't have all the answers. I firmly believe in embodying the change I want to see in the world, and I recognise that organisations reflect the style and values of their leaders. While I'm confident that many embrace, the core philosophy of 'no dogma' and 'treating people as talent'. I understand that the complete cycle of change may not be universally adopted. Nonetheless, creating an environment where individuals can bring their authentic selves to work is a worthwhile goal in itself.

That's the beauty of inspiring and influential leadership. I recognise that I can't force people to enjoy the music, but I believe that this style is contagious. As people witness and experience its positive impact, they often find themselves tapping their feet and eventually joining in the dance.

Frequently Asked Questions

I have had the chance to share my thoughts with the talented people at Criterion, but also with the wider world:

- the CIPD mission launch in London the IDEXX Leadership Development Programme.
- the Game Developers Conference in San Francisco.
- the Guildford Game festival in the UK.
- Polo Digital de Manaus, Brazil.
- The Games Gathering in Kiev.
- Pocket Gamer conference in London.

I have met amazing, passionate people that I have learned so much from. The questions below are ones that have come up most often in the discussions I have had in offices, conference halls, meeting rooms, bars, and restaurants.

It sounds really passive; that will not work for my situation.

People sometimes hear 'servant leadership' and think of something really passive; maybe it means giving away our power. I think I worried about that in the early stages of the journey. I have found that, in fact, as my leadership style emerged, it meant stepping fully into my power.

Many fundamental things about leadership have stayed the same: the need to be fully committed, the need to bring my passion for what I do, identifying and focusing on what I am working on towards a motivational purpose, and of course, the ever-present need to manage change. What changes is the mindset and style of leadership that I have tried to describe here.

What should I do when I find myself in victim space?

First of all, congratulations on your self-awareness!

To notice this is no small feat.

We know what we *shouldn't* be doing in this space. Leading from any of these leadership mindsets will have the effect of bringing more people into that space. Also, we know that we can cause ourselves more suffering by trying to deny, suppress, or resist the painful emotions that lead us into victim space.

So, what is the work here? To minimise the suffering, we need to disidentify from the absolute thoughts and negative feelings of this phase without denying them. So, we accept that we are feeling sad, lonely, isolated, angry, or frustrated, and we notice that we are thinking that some negative event means nothing can ever be any good again. However, we recognise that those feelings are not us, and those thoughts are just thoughts we are thinking; they do not define us.

How happy should I expect to be?

As a side note here, it is worth noting that in western societies, the message is directly and subtly transmitted that happiness is our goal and we should be happy all the time. I believe this is a dangerous misdirection that actually promotes unhappiness.

It is not even physically possible to be happy all the time. In the research first published in 1971, two psychologists, Brickman, and Campbell, described the 'hedonic treadmill'. Their research showed that humans have a process of hedonic adaptation where, over the longer term, happiness returns to a set point regardless of major positive or negative events. So regardless of winning the lottery or losing a limb, our happiness tends to return to this same set point. Setting permanent happiness as a goal, therefore, is setting yourself up for failure, disappointment, and (perhaps ironically) unhappiness.

In his book 'The Antidote: Happiness for People Who Can't Stand Positive Thinking' Oliver Burke describes, with reference to historical and contemporary examples, how an oblique approach towards happiness may lead to greater contentment and fulfilment.

I am not led this way; how can I start?

There is an excellent TED talk on influence by Jim Rohn, "You are the average of the 5 people you spend the most time with." So, there is a decision to be made if you are spending time at work with people you want to be influenced by. Equally, there is at least one person you lead who spends the most time with you. Start with that person; the effect could be contagious! Furthermore, if you go back to practicing, personal authenticity, if this is truly you, you may well find it impossible to lead any other way.

Regarding autonomy over the team, do people get locked into a project for a certain amount of time, no switching between projects, etc.?

There are times when business priorities come up and people have to move. People often think that once they're in a game, they're on it to ship.

Audio and UI might be like 'craft service' and they operate mostly self-contained. The Criterion audio team call them, 'scouts' that go out to teams.

Sounds compelling. Why aren't there more people leading this way? What stops people?

I believe that choosing to lead this way is a choice as much about the way we want to live it is about the way we want to work. In the west, in particular, we live in a society that encourages noisy ego, and encourages a scarcity mindset; the message that you never have enough and, by extension, are never enough prevalent in all forms of media, especially advertising. I believe it takes something significant in life to start us on the journey of self-discovery. So far, for me, despite searching, I have not seen that thing as something other than trauma. It is why I chose the quote from the Tao Te Ching at the start of this book: "If you want to become whole, then first let yourself be broken." If you find something else, please let me know!

As a servant leader. How do you keep everyone's problem from becoming your problem?

This is one that has been the focus of much inquiry and work for me. The key I have found is the distinction between what the people who lead need and what they want. Your job is to get them what they need. What they don't need is for you to take their burden, be it personal or professional, from them. They cannot grow if you do that. Your job is to get them what they need to be effective; this may be removing roadblocks for them, but it is more often context, feedback, alignment with others on the team, and compassionate truth.

Do you have tips for a situation where you keep arguing with someone over what to do next?

Well, this is a good opportunity to practice your listening skills. Remember, most people never listen; they are just waiting to speak. Bring some curiosity to the other person's position; why do they believe what they appear to believe? Do you know what they are proposing?

Remember, discussing benefits does not work. Discussing the benefits you want to achieve has a much greater chance of being productive than arguing over the work you want to do.

If you can solve the difference of opinion with a quick prototype of another practical test, then do that!

How do you know when to give up on someone?

As a leader who believes in and trusts their people, it is a risk to carry on too long with someone who is not right for our organisation. Let's assume this is not a case of being incompetent at a core hard skill of the job (it rarely is, as that is the easiest thing to filter on at an interview). For me, there are two checks:

- Is this person's continuing struggle creating unacceptable suffering for the rest of the team? I serve the team best by removing that person.
- Does this person oppose one of our organisation's core values? The values have to be non-negotiable; that is, we don't need everyone to be

100% convinced by all of them, but they cannot hold the opposing value and continue in the organisation.

How do you manage if you have to give your team bad news?

Two things are really important here. First, you need to get ahead of your team in processing bad news. You need an appropriate amount of time, be it a few days or a few weeks, to work through your own reaction before you attempt to lead a team through theirs. Secondly, when you do stand in front of your team, you need to be resourceful. Spend some time to fuel yourself physically, emotionally, and mentally before you step into that particular arena.

As parents of boys, what can we do to help them with their vulnerability?

As parents, I believe we do no one (ourselves, each other, our kids) service by blaming anyone, least of all ourselves. We are very much all in this together.

We have to look for all the ways we can communicate to our kids, but especially to our boys, that it is ok to be vulnerable and that they are loved unconditionally no matter what they do or don't achieve in anything. As Danielle Laporte put it, "You're not going to die. Here's the white-hot truth: if you go bankrupt, you'll still be okay. If you lose the gig, the lover, or the house, you'll still be okay. If you sing off-key, get beat by the competition, have your heart shattered, get fired…it's not going to kill you. Ask anyone who's been through it."

That, believe it or not, is what I think of as the easy part.

Perhaps the harder part, as dads, is that we have to model vulnerability. What does that look like? To riff off Brene Brown again, then it is things like the willingness to say, 'I love you' first…the willingness to do something where there are no guarantees, or the willingness to invest in a relationship that may or may not work out. I would add the willingness to say what you really think and the willingness to ask for what you need.

I am still working on this. I am not great at apologising, for instance, because it feels vulnerable.

I am not in a leadership position; how can I practice liberated leadership?

You are not your job title. Can you find a way to let go of the idea that "my job title should change before I do?" If we wait for something outside to change us or define us, we give away power and can stay locked in victim space.

My favourite answer to "How do you know if you are a leader?" is "Look behind you; is anyone following you?" You can start to develop yourself and practice the Liberated Leadership change cycle on yourself, and before you know it, people will be following you.

The anointment and job title will follow.

I have been given feedback that I need to make things simpler.

It's very hard to get to something simple...it is not as if we consciously reject that choice...although egoistic leaders often express their needs this way! A good question I still ask myself regularly is, "Is this complex because I am making it complex or because it is intrinsically complex?"

Simple is not the lowest-cost or lowest-friction option. Consider you have a stick to store in the stock pile. The stock pile is a complex, entangled mess. The lowest-cost, lowest-friction thing to do is throw the stick on top of the pile. The pile of sticks is not "simple." You'd have to design a stick taxonomy, sort the sticks, and create, test, and implement 'stick-adding' UX. But your job as a liberated leader is to ask the question, "Why are we collecting sticks? What benefit do we expect to derive?" With the answer to that we can prioritise and work with experts to achieve that benefit with the least effort.

As Leonador Da Vinicio said,"Simplicity is the ultimate sophistication."

What is the biggest fear you have had to overcome on the road to liberated leadership?

I've been on a journey of confronting and overcoming my fear of death and dying. It took some time for me to realise that resisting this fear only drained my energy without truly addressing it. It was only when I made significant breakthroughs in other core beliefs that I felt ready to face the underlying beliefs fuelling this fear.

During a powerful session with my coach, I identified a core belief that "there is nothing after death." Holding onto this belief left me feeling desolate, scared, overwhelmed, and disconnected. However, when asked if I truly knew this belief to be true, I had to admit that I couldn't absolutely know for sure. That realisation opened up the possibility of letting go.

In further reflection and practice, it became clear that the answer might be as simple as accepting the unknown. I no longer needed to find a concrete answer to what happens after death, a question that has perplexed even great minds. This realisation marked a significant moment in my personal development. Accepting that I didn't know the answer allowed the fear to diminish over time until it eventually disappeared completely.

It's been a transformative journey, learning to let go of the need for certainty and embracing the acceptance of the unknown.

Steve Jobs' words from his Stanford commencement speech resonate with me. "Remembering that you are going to die is the best way I know to avoid the trap of thinking you have something to lose. You are already naked. There is no reason not to follow your heart."

You suffered from burnout, making games called Burnout. Do you believe in nominative determinism?

Honestly, I don't really believe in nominative determinism, the idea that our names somehow shape our destinies. However, I do believe that every game we create is a reflection of who we are as game developers. Our experiences, emotions, and perspectives inevitably find their way into the games we make.

On a related note, I've always been captivated by Carl Jung's theory of synchronicity describes those intriguing 'meaningful coincidences' that seem to happen in our lives. It's a concept that has fascinated me since I first encountered it as a teenager. It's amazing how certain events or connections can carry profound significance and seem to go beyond mere chance.

Given the focus on being present, what is your view on planning because it necessarily brings us into the future and away from the present?

Planning with presence is all about keeping our focus on the present moment and not getting too caught up in the end goal. We have to be mindful of the decisions we truly need to make right now, understanding the difference between what's important and what's urgent. Sometimes we feel like we need to make decisions on everything, but in reality, some things can be put on hold until we have a clearer picture of our game and how it's evolving. It's important to have a vision of what we're creating, but as we learn more about the game, we adapt and refine our understanding of it. So, it's not about planning less, but rather planning to adapt and adjust. We shouldn't waste our time creating a detailed Gantt chart that maps out a single version of the future because, let's face it, things rarely go exactly as planned. Better to put your energy into being clear about priorities for what needs to be done now, a route to your destination, and early warning systems that rerouting is required.

References

Adams, Douglas. (2020) *The Hitchhiker's Guide to the Galaxy: Hitchhiker's Guide to the Galaxy Book 1: 42nd Anniversary Edition*. N.p.: Pan Macmillan.

Brown, Brené. (2019) *Dare to Lead: Brave Work. Tough Conversations. Whole Hearts*. N.p.: Diversified Publishing.

Brown, Brené. (2019) *Dare to Lead: Brave Work. Tough Conversations. Whole Hearts*. N.p.: Diversified Publishing.

Burkeman, Oliver. (2018) *The Antidote: Happiness for People Who Can't Stand Positive Thinking*. N.p.: Penguin Random House.

Cantopher, Tim. (2012) *Depressive Illness: The Curse of the Strong*. N.p.: Sheldon.

Cantopher, Tim. (2012) *Depressive Illness: The Curse of the Strong*. N.p.: Sheldon.

Cantopher, Tim. (2019) *Stress Related Illness*. N.p.: Mobius.

Coelho, Paulo. (1995) *The Alchemist*. Translated by Alan R. Clarke. N.p.: HarperCollins.

Edmondson, Amy C. (2018) *The Fearless Organization: Creating Psychological Safety in the Workplace for Learning, Innovation, and Growth*. N.p.: Wiley.

Gilovich, Thomas, Victoria Husted Medvec, and K. V. Savitsky. (2000) "The spotlight effect in social judgment: An egocentric bias in estimates of the salience of one's own actions and appearance." *Journal of Personality and Social Psychology* 78 (2): 211–222. https://doi.org/10.1037/0022-3514.78.2.211.

Goleman, Daniel. n.d. "What Makes a Leader?" *Harvard Business Review,* 76:93–102.

Hemingway, Ernest. (1994) *Across the River and into the Trees (Arrow Classic).* N.p.: Arrow.

Hendricks, Gay, and Kathlyn Hendricks. (1990) *Conscious Loving: The Journey to Co-Commitment.* N.p.: Random House Publishing Group.

Hendricks, Gay, and Kathlyn Hendricks. (1990) *Conscious Loving: The Journey to Co-Commitment.* N.p.: Random House Publishing Group.

Hendricks, Kathlyn, and Gay Hendricks. (1990) *Conscious Loving: The Journey to Co-Commitment.* N.p.: Random House Publishing Group.

Ibarra, Professor Herminia. n.d. *The Authenticityn Paradox.* https://youtu.be/CIjI3TmEzrs.

Kabat-Zinn, Jon, Chade-Meng Tan, and Daniel Goleman. (2012) *Search Inside Yourself.* N.p.: HarperCollins.

Kayes, D. C. (2006) *Destructive Goal Pursuit: The Mt. Everest Disaster.* N.p.: Palgrave Macmillan.

Kerr, Robert, John Garvin, Norma Heaton, and Emily Boyle. 2. "Emotional intelligence and leadership effectiveness." *Leadership & Organization Development Journal* 27 (4): 265–279.

Laozi, and Stephen Addiss. (1993) *Tao Te Ching.* Translated by Stephen Addiss and Stanley Lombardo. N.p.: Hackett Publishing Company.

Pink, Daniel H. (2018) *Drive: The Surprising Truth about what Motivates Us.* N.p.: Canongate Books.

Sakulku, J. (2011) "The Impostor Phenomenon." *The Journal of Behavioural Science* 6 (1). https://doi.org/10.14456/ijbs.2011.6.

Singer, Tania, and Olga M. Kilmecki. (22 September 2014) *Empathy and Compassion.* Vol. 24, Issue 24.
https://www.sciencedirect.com/science/journ al/09609822/24/18.

Tolle, Eckhart. (2001) *The Power of Now: A Guide to Spiritual Enlightenment.* N.p.: Hodder and Stoughton.

Tzu, Lao, and Stephen Addiss. (1993) *Tao Te Ching.* Translated by Stephen Addiss and Stanley Lombardo. N.p.: Hackett Publishing Company.

Tzu, Lao, and McDonald. (2010) *Tao Te Ching.* Translated by John H. McDonald. N.p.: Arcturus Publishing.

Williams, Mark, and Danny Penman. (2011) *Mindfulness: A Practical Guide to Finding Peace in a Frantic World.* N.p.: Piatkus.

Wilson, Timothy D., David A. Reinhart, Erin C. Westgate, Daniel T. Gilbert, Nicole Ellerbeck, Cheryl Hahn, Casey L. Brown, and Adi Shaked. (2014) "Just think: The challenges of the disengaged mind." *Science* 345, no. 6192 (July): 75–77. https://www.science.org/doi/10.1126/science.1250830.

Printed in Great Britain
by Amazon

48150027R00077